D0007087

Date Due

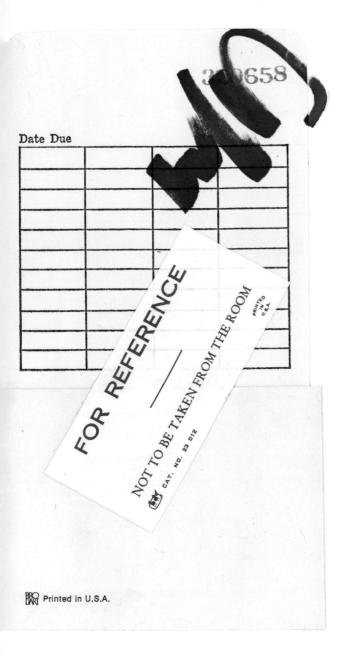

FOR REFERENCE

NOT TO BE TAKEN FROM THE ROOM

PRINTED IN U.S.A.

CAT. NO. 23 012

Early English Hymns: An Index

by

EDNA D. PARKS

The Scarecrow Press, Inc.
Metuchen, N.J.   1972

Copyright 1972 by Edna D. Parks

Library of Congress Cataloging in Publication Data

Parks, Edna D
  Early English hymns.

    1. Hymns, English--Indexes. I. Title.
BV305.P37   016.7839   72-753
ISBN 0-8108-0483-2

TABLE OF CONTENTS

iii

PREFACE

The index of hymns assembled here is the result of investigation of the widely held idea that hymn writing in English dates from Isaac Watts (1674-1748), the so-called "Father of English Hymnody." The investigation proved the idea false, at least to this writer, and because so many of the hymns found are not listed in Julian's Dictionary of Hymnology, nor are they gathered together in any one source, it seemed of value to make the index.

It is true that some of the religious poetry of the 17th-century poets cited here was not conceived as congregational song but because much which was suitable was soon adapted and joined with a tune, it is included. Some poems which were not set to music are included if they conformed to the definition of hymn which was used for the investigation. A hymn was distinguished from a Psalm and from paraphrased scripture. It expressed praise or prayer to God, calls to his service, or commented on his purpose in man's life. The poetry was original and simple enough to be useful for congregational singing when set to music.

It was my intention to exclude carols from the index because of already existing collections of them. However, the distinction between hymns and carols is often difficult to make and some questions may arise about omissions or inclusions of this genre.

Hymns are arranged in alphabetical order by first line; On the second line of the entry, comes 1) the meter; 2) the number of stanzas or lines found in the earliest publication of the poetry; and 3) the name of the author. (Amen or Allelujah is included on this line in those rare instances when it was printed in the source.) The third line of the entry gives the date of the publication and the number and/ or page where the hymn was located. Information about the tune is on the following line with composer's name, when known, at the far right. It should be noted that both meter and number of stanzas were frequently changed when the hymn was joined with a tune. The earliest date that the hymn was joined with a tune has been sought, and there has been no attempt to discover how many different tunes may have been used with the hymn after that date. If there was a statement in a publication that the hymns were to be sung, but no tunes printed, this information is supplied in the entry. Such publications frequently are used to supply the earliest date for the joining of a hymn with a tune even though no specific tune can be cited. Probably these hymns were sung to the Common Tunes found in the Psalters.

Information in entries marked * is taken from the Julian Dictionary of Hymnology. Information in entries marked ** was found in the publication cited in the entry. Information in all the other entries has been verified in the original publication.

Edna D. Parks
Wakefield, Massachusetts
May, 1971

v

ABBREVIATIONS

B. M.	British Museum
C. H. C. G.	A Collection of Hymns of the Children of God in All Ages
Ch. Sc. of Praise	The Christian Sacrifice of Praise for the Use of the Religious Society of Romney
C. M.	Common meter
C. M. D.	Common meter double
Contemplations	Sir Matthew Hale, Contemplations Moral and Divine
D.	Double
Devotions	John Austin, Devotions. First Part in the Antient Way of Offices
Devot. ed. H.	George Hickes, ed., Devotions in the Ancient Way of Offices with Psalms, Hymns and Prayers
Farr	E. Farr, ed., Select Poetry Chiefly Devotional
Foundery	A Collection of Tunes, Set to Music As they are Commonly Sung at the Foundery
Hal.	George Wither, Halelviah
Hendee	A Collection of Psalms and Hymns for Christian Worship
Hymns and Songs	George Wither, The Hymns and Songs of the Church

Hys. for Christian Ch. and Hm.	James Martineau, ed., Hymns for the Christian Church and Home
Hys. in Commem.	Joseph Stennett, Hymns in Commemoration of the Sufferings of Our Blessed Saviour Jesus Christ Compos'd for the Celebration of His Holy Supper
Hys. of the P. E. Church	Hymns of the Protestant Episcopal Church in the United States of America, Boston, 1828.
$\ell(\ell)$.	Line(s)
L. M.	Long meter
L. M. D.	Long meter double
Palgrave	Francis T. Palgrave, ed., The Treasury of Sacred Song
Ps. and Hys. Asylum	Psalms and Hymns for the Use of the Chapel of the Asylum for Female Orphans
Sacred Poetry	Jeremy Belknap, ed., Sacred Poetry Consisting of Psalms and Hymns Adapted to Christian Devotion...
St. Martin's	The Psalms and Hymns usually Sung in the Churches and Tabernacles of St. Martin's in the Fields, and St. James's Westminster
St. Peter's Complaint	Robert Southwell, Saint Peter's Complaint, Mary Magdalen's Tears, with Other Works of the Author

The second Booke	The second Booke of the Musicke of M. William Damon
S. M.	Short meter
S. M. D.	Short meter double
S. P. C. K.	Society for Promoting Christian Knowledge
st(s).	Stanza(s)
Tate and Brady	A New Version of the Psalms of David by N. Tate and N. Brady together with some hymns...[by] J. Stennett, Is. Watts, S. Browne and J. Mason
10 Com.	Ten Commandments
Trinity Church	Hymns Selected from the Most Approved Authors for the Use of Trinity Church, Boston

INDEX

1623 Hymns and Songs, No. LIV, p. 42
Tune in same volume: Song 9   Orlando Gibbons

9.   A house I had (a heart I mean) so wide
10. 10. 10. 10. 10. 10. 10 (15 sts.) [Christopher Harvey]
1640 The Synagogue, pp. 15-18
1754 C. H. C. G. , Part I, No. 382, p. 22
8. 8. 8. 8. 10. 10   9 sts.
Tune to be selected by meter from appended
Table of Metres and Tunes

10.   A hymn to God the Father
See: Hear me, O God!   Ben. Johnson [sic]

11.   A living stream as crystal clear
See: My soul doth magnify the   John Mason
Lord

12.   A song of joy unto the Lord we sing
10. 10. 10. 10. 10   6 sts.   George Wither
10. 10 refrain
1623 Hymns and Songs, No. XLVII, p. 38
Tune in same volume: Song 47   Orlando Gibbons

13.   A soul that's burden'd with the weight
C. M. D.   4 sts.   [Thomas Shepherd]
1693 Penetential Cries, No. XXVI, p. 40
No tune given but intended to be sung

14.   A sov'raigntie, though some obtain
C. M. D.   5 sts.   George Wither
1641 Hal. Pt. 3, No. III, pp. 354-356
Suggested tune: Psalm 4

15.   A thousand perils, ev'ry day
C. M. D.   3 sts.   George Wither
1641 Hal. Pt. 1, No. CVIII, pp. 212-213
Suggested tune: Psalm 4

16.   A time so cursed once was here
C. M. D.   4 sts.   George Wither
1641 Hal. Pt. 1, No. LXXXIII, pp. 158-159
Suggested tune: Psalm 22

17.   A winged harbinger from bright heav'n flown
irreg.   24 ℓ ℓ.; Allelujah; Amen   Jeremy Taylor
1655 Festival Hymns appended to The
Golden Grove, p. 163

18.   Accept, O God, my holy fires
            8. 8. 8. 8. 8. 8. 8   John Quarles
        1663 Divine Meditations... with... Divine
        Ejaculations, p. 133

19.   **Adam comes forth; but in a new edition
         **10. 8. 8. 10   3 sts.   [Faithfull Teate]
        1754 C. H. C. G., Part 1, No. 386, p. 225
        Tune to be selected by meter from appended
        Table of Metres and Tunes

20.   Adieu, dear Lord, I kiss your sacred feet
         irreg.   4 sts.   Lancelot Addison
        1699 Devotional Poems, pp. 23-24
        1754 C. H. C. G., Part I, No. 496, pp. 290-291
        Begins: "Farewell, dear Lord, I kiss
          your sacred feet"
        Tune to be selected by meter from
          appended Table of Metres and Tunes

21.   Adieu, dear Lord, if you'll ascend from me
         10. 10. 10. 10   5 sts.   Lancelot Addison
        1699 Devotional Poems, pp. 25-26
        1754 C. H. C. G., Part I, No. 498, p. 291
        10. 10   3 sts.
        st. 2, ℓ. 1: "Oh what is't Lord, that
          you would have me do"
        Tune to be selected by meter from
          appended Table of Metres and Tunes

22.   Adieu, dear master, we must part I see
         irreg.   22 ℓℓ.   Lancelot Addison
        1699 Devotional Poems, pp. 19-20
        1754 C. H. C. G., Part I, No. 497, p. 291
        Begins: "Farewell, dear master, we
          must part I see"
        Tune to be selected by meter from
          appended Table of Metres and Tunes

23.   *Again our weekly labours end
         See: Another six days   Joseph Stennett

24.   **Ah conscience! conscience! when I look
         **8. 8. 8. 4. D.   5 sts.   [Faithfull Teate]
        1754 C. H. C. G., Part I, No. 391, pp. 228-229
        Tune to be selected by meter from
          appended Table of Metres and Tunes

25.   Ah helpless wretch! what shall I do
            C. M.   9 sts.   William Hunnis
            1597 The Poor Widowes Mite, bound with Seven
                 Sobs of a Sorrowful Soule for Sinne, pp. 31-
                 32
            Tune in same volume   William Hunnis

26.   Ah! Lord, Ah! Lord, what have I done
            C. M. D.   4 sts.   [John Mason]
            1693 Penetential Cries, No. I, p. 4
            No tune given but intended to be sung

27.   Ah me! my heart's the seat of war
            C. M. D.   3 sts.   Thomas Shepherd
            C. M.   1 st.
            1743 Penetential Cries, No. XIX
            No tune given but intended to be sung

28.   Ah me! where may I seek a friend
            C. M. D.   10 sts.   George Wither
            1641 Hal. Pt. 1, No. LXXVIII, pp. 144-146
            Suggested tune: Psalm 43

29.   Ah, my dear Lord! what couldst thou spy
            See: Lord, when thou didst   Henry Vaughan
               thyself undress

30.   **Ah, on my saviour's tender flesh
            See: Sorrow betide my   [Christopher Harvey]
               sins! must smart so soon

31.   Aid me, O Lord my God, for there be three
            10 decasyllables 18 sts.   Thomas Heywood
            1635 The Hierarchie of the Blessed Angells, pp.
                 488-493

32.   Alack when I look back
            S. M. D. ; 8.8.6.8. (2 sts. ; Amen) William Hunnis
            1597 A Lamentation bound with Comfortable Dia-
                 logs, pp. 67-68
            Tune in same volume   William Hunnis

33.   Alas! for I have seen the Lord
            C. M. D.   4 sts.   [John Mason]
            C. M.   1 st.
            1693 Penetential Cries, No. III, p. 6
            No tune given but intended to be sung

34.   Alas, my God that we should be
                C. M. D.   6 sts.   [Thomas Shepherd]
                1693 Penetential Cries, No. XXIX, p. 43
                    st. 4, ℓ. 1: "When wilt thou come unto me
                        Lord"
                    st. 4, ℓ. 5: "When wilt thou come unto me
                        Lord"
                    st. 6, ℓ. 1: "When wilt thou come unto me
                        Lord"
                No tune given but intended to be sung

35.   Alas! my heart, what meanest thou
                C. M. D.   11 sts.   George Wither
                1641 Hal. Pt. I, No. CXI, pp. 218-221
                Suggested tune: Te Deum

36.   Alas! my Lord is going
                7. 3. 7. 3. 7. 3. 7. 3. 8. 8.(3 sts.)[Christopher Harvey]
                1640 The Synagogue, p. 9

37.   All glory unto God
                S. M. D.   4 sts.   Abraham Fleming
                1608 The Diamond of Devotion, pp. 257-258

38.   *All human succours now are flown
                *1721 Hymns for all Festivals of   Thomas Ken
                    the Year

39.   All people praise the Lord
                S. M.   7 sts.   Abraham Fleming
                1608 The Diamond of Devotion, pp. 253-254

40.   All praise and glory that we may
                C. M. D.   5 sts.   George Wither
                1623 Hymns and Songs, No. LXXXI, p. 56
                Tune in same volume: Song 3 Orlando Gibbons

41.   *All praise to thee in light arrayed
                See: My God, now I from   Thomas Ken
                    sleep awake

42.   All praise to thee my God, this night
                L. M.   11 sts. ; Doxology   Thomas Ken
                *1674 Sung at Winchester College
                *1692 Pamphlet with no title page, printed for
                    Rich. Smith
                1693 Harmonia Sacra, Bk. 2, with tune, pp. 29-
                    34   Jeremiah Clarke

See Julian's <u>Dictionary of Hymnology</u> for lengthy
discussion of publication and revision.

43.   *All praise to thee who safe hast kept
          See: Awake my soul, and with   Thomas Ken
             the sun

44.   All this is just, Lord, I confess
          L. M.   6 sts.   Richard Baxter
          1861 <u>Poetical Fragments</u>, pp. 77-78
          Suggested tune: <u>Psalm 51</u>

45.   All the created works, O Lord
          C. M.   8 sts.   Joseph Stennett
          1697 <u>Hys. in Commen.</u>, No. XXV, p. 32
          No tune given but intended to be sung

46.   All you that fear the Lord, give ear
          C. M.   28 sts.   Benjamin Keach
          1681 <u>Sion in Distress</u>, 2nd ed., pp. 123-128

47.   Almighty God, how hast thou born
          C. M. D.   4 sts.   John Mason
          C. M.   1 st.
          1683 <u>Spiritual Songs</u>, No. XXI, pp. 46-47
          No tune given but intended to be sung

48.   Almighty God, when he had raised the frame
          76 decasyllables   Sir Matthew Hale
          1676 <u>Contemplations</u>, "Poems upon Christmas
             <u>Day</u>," No. 1, (written in 1651) pp. 501-503
          ℓ. 23 is: "But man rebels, and for one tast
             doth choose"

49.   Although he knows it putrifies
          L. M. D.   6 sts.   George Wither
          1641 <u>Hal.</u> Pt. 2, No. XIX, pp. 266-267
          Suggested tune: <u>10 Com.</u>

50.   Although, my God! that sacrifice
          C. M. D.   4 sts.   George Wither
          1641 <u>Hal.</u> Pt. 1, No. XLIX, pp. 81-82
          Suggested tune: <u>Psalm 101</u>

51.   Although that hope is frustrate made
          C. M. D.   5 sts.   George Wither
          1641 <u>Hal.</u> Pt. 1, No. CVII, pp. 210-211
          Suggested tune: <u>Psalm 4</u>

52.   Although transgressors, Lord, we be
               L. M. D.   8 sts.   George Wither
           1641 Hal. Pt. 1, No. LXI, pp. 114-116
           Suggested tune: Lamentation

53.   Amid so many miseries
               C. M.   7 sts.   Abraham Fleming
           1608 The Diamond of Devotion, pp. 267-269

54.   Among the Jews let every tribe
               C. M. D.   5 sts.   [Thomas Shepherd]
               C. M.   1 st.
           1693 Penetential Cries, No. XXIV, p. 37
           No tune given but intended to be sung

55.   Among these blessings which on me
               C. M. D.   4 sts.   George Wither
           1641 Hal. Pt. 3, No. XVI, pp. 381-382
           Suggested tune: Psalm 4

56.   Among those points of neighbourhood
               L. M. D.   7 sts.   George Wither
           1641 Hal. Pt. 1, No. XLIII, pp. 70-72
           No tune given but intended to be sung

57.   Among those wonders here on earth
               L. M. D.   5 sts.   George Wither
           1641 Hal. Pt. 1, No. XLVII, pp. 78-79
           Suggested tune: 10 Com.

58.   An humble heart, O God
               S. M.   7 sts.   Abraham Fleming
           1608 The Diamond of Devotion, pp. 262-263

59.   And art thou come, blest Babe, and come to me?
               irreg.   4 sts.   Lancelot Addison
           1699 Devotional Poems, pp. 2-4
               st. 3, ℓ. 1: "Here let me sigh"
           1754 C. H. C. G., Part I, No. 482, p. 281
               10.10   3 sts.
           Tune to be selected by meter from appended
               Table of Metres and Tunes

60.   And art thou grieved, sweet and sacred dove
               10. 4. 4. 10. 8. 8   6 sts.   George Herbert
           1633 The Temple, pp. 128-129
           1688 Harmonia Sacra, with tune,   John Blow
               pp. 27-29

61.   And art thou parting, dearest Lord, to go
              irreg.   3 sts.   Lancelot Addison
         1699 Devotional Poems, pp. 11-12

62.   And do we then believe
              S. M.   8 sts.; Amen   John Austin
         1672 (1st ed. 1668) Devotions, No. XVI, p. 141
         1701 Devot. ed. H., p. 183; tune in separate
              section

63.   And dost thou come, O blessed Lord
              See: I sojourn in a vale of tears   John Mason

64.   And may I yet, dear Lord, be dear to you
              10.10.10.10   6 sts.   Lancelot Addison
         1699 Devotional Poems, pp. 53-54

65.   And now, my soul, canst thou forget
              L. M.   8 sts.; Amen   John Austin
         1672 (1st ed. 1668) Devotions, No. XXIII, pp.
              203-204
         1701 Devot. ed. H., p. 268; tune p. 2 in sepa-
              rate section

66.   **And now ye day which in ye morn was thine
              **10.10.10.10   5 sts.   Joseph Beaumont
         c.1643 Minor Poems, MS.
         1914 Reprint, p. 35

67.   And shall I drown the man, and drench the beast
              irreg.   4 sts.   Lancelot Addison
         1699 Devotional Poems, pp. 66-67

68.   Another six days' work is done
              L. M.   14 sts.   Joseph Stennett
         *1732 Works Vol. IV, pp. 231-234
            *Sung before his death in 1713
         *1769 Ash and Evans' Bristol Baptist Coll., with
              tune
              Suggested tune: Any L. M. tune
              *Variants: "Again our weekly labours end"
                        "Another week its course has run"
                        "Return, my soul, enjoy thy rest"

69.   *Another week its course has run
              See: Another six days' work   Joseph Stennett

70. **Armies of angels myriads of saints
              **14 decasyllables   Barnaby Barnes
        **1595 A Divine Centurie of Spirituall Sonnets
              1815 Reprint, p. 38

71. As Blessed Andrew on a day
              L. M. D.   3 sts.   George Wither
        1623 Hymns and Songs, No. LXI, p. 46
        Tune in same volume: Song 44 Orlando Gibbons

72. As due by many titles I resign
              14 decasyllables   John Donne
        1633 Poems, Holy Sonnet, No. I, p. 32
        ℓ ℓ . 2 & 3: "Myself to thee, O God, first I
              was made
              By thee, and for thee, and when I was de-
              cay'd"
        1754 C. H. C. G., Part I, No. 383, pp. 222-223
        10. 10. 10. 10   14 sts.
        Begins: "Thou hast made me: and shall thy
              work decay"
        Tune to be selected by meter from appended
        Table of Metres and Tunes

73. *As earth's pageant passes by
              *Condensed from "Home"   Joseph Beaumont
        *1749 Original Poems in English and Latin, p. 8

74. As e're I down am couched there
              C. M. D.   5 sts.   George Wither
        1641 Hal. Pt. 1, No. XIX, pp. 28-29
        Suggested tune: Psalm 33 or 34

75. As he that sees a dark and shady grove
              10. 10. 10. 10. 10. 10 3 sts.   George Herbert
        1633 The Temple, p. 36
        1754 C. H. C. G., Pt. I, No. 356, p. 213
        10. 10. 10. 10   3 sts. + 2 decasyllables
        Tune to be selected by meter from appended
        Table of Metres and Tunes

76. **As I in hoary winter's night stood shivering in the snow
              **16 fourteeners   Robert Southwell
        **1634 St. Peter's Complaint
              1856 Reprint, pp. 98-99

77. **As those three kings, touch'd with a sacred zeal

**14 decasyllables   Barnaby Barnes
**1595 A Divine Centurie of Spirituall Sonnets
 1815 Reprint, p. 39

78.   As travellers when the twilight's come
          L. M.   7 sts.   Henry Vaughan
       1650 Silex Scintillans, pp. 88-89

79.   As we by water wash away
          C. M. D.   3 sts.   George Wither
       1641 Hal. Pt. 1, No. VI, pp. 10-11
        Suggested tunes: Psalm 1, 4 or 30

80.   Attend, O Lord, and hear
          See: Give ear, O Lord   William Hunnis

81.   Attend ye nations and give ear
          C. M.   7 sts.   Abraham Fleming
       1608 The Diamond of Devotion, pp. 272-273

82.   Awake, glad heart! get up, and sing
          8. 8. 4. 4. 8. 8   5 sts.   Henry Vaughan
       1650 Silex Scintillans, pp. 61-62

83.   Awake my love, awake my joy
          See: Now from the altar of my   John Mason
                heart

84.   Awake my soul, and with the sun
          L. M.   13 sts.; Doxology Thomas Ken
        *1674 Sung at Winchester College
        *1692 Pamphlet with no title page, printed for
              Rich. Smith

85. **Awake my soul, awake and see
          See: Open thine eyes my soul,   John Austin
                and see

86.   Awake my soul, awake mine eyes!
          18 octosyllables and 10.10   Thomas Flatman
       1674 Poems and Songs, pp. 47-48
       1701 The Divine Companion, with   Jer. Clarke
            tune, p. 29

87.   Awake my soul, chase from thine eyes
          8. 8. 6. 8. 8. 6   7 sts.; Amen   John Austin
       1672 (1st ed. 1668) Devotions, No. XXXVI, pp.

321-322
1701 <u>Devot. ed. H.</u>, p. 440; tune p. 10 separate
section

88.   Awake O soul, and look abroad
        L. M.   18 sts.   Richard Smyth
      1634 <u>Munition Against Mans Misery</u>, precedes
         <u>p. 1</u>

89.   Awake sad heart, whom sorrow ever drowns
        10. 8. 10. 8. 4. 10. 10. 10   2 sts. George Herbert
      1633 <u>The Temple</u>, pp. 104-105
      1754 <u>C. H. C. G.</u>, Pt. I, No. 360, p. 214
        8. 8. 8. 8. 10. 10   2 sts.
      Tune to be selected by meter from appended
      <u>Table of Metres and Tunes</u>

90.   Away dark thoughts, awake my joy
        C. M. D.   4 sts.   John Mason
      1683 <u>Spiritual Songs</u>, No. XII
      No tune given but intended to be sung

91.   Away despair; my gracious Lord doth hear
        10. 8. 8. 8. 8. 10   George Herbert
      1633 <u>The Temple</u>, pp. 145-146
        st. 2, ℓ. 1: "Hast not heard, that Lord Jesus
        dy'd"
      1754 <u>C. H. C. G.</u>, Pt. I, No. 375, p. 219
      Begins with st. 2 of above.
      Tune to be selected by meter from appended
      <u>Table of Metres and Tunes</u>

92. **Be fervent in the truth
        **6. 6. 6. 6. D.   2 sts.   [Robert Smith?]
      1754 <u>C. H. C. G.</u>, Pt. I, No. 351, p. 212
      Tune to be selected by meter from appended
      <u>Table of Metres and Tunes</u>

93.   Be gracious, Lord, unto my grief
        8. 8. 8. 8. 8. 8   John Quarles
      1663 <u>Divine Meditations... With... Divine Ejacula-
      tions</u>, p. 145

94.   Be thou my trust, my God, and I
        8. 8. 8. 8. 8. 8   John Quarles
      1663 <u>Divine Meditations... With... Divine Ejacula-
      tions</u>, p. 139

95.   Because the world might not pretend
               8. 8. 8. 8. 8. 8   6 sts.   George Wither
               1623 Hymns and Songs, No. LXXI, p. 50
               Tune in same volume: Song 9   Orlando Gibbons

96.   Before my face the picture hangs
               8. 8. 8. 8. 8. 8   9 sts.   Robert Southwell
               1634 Maeoniae, pp. 136-138

97.   Before there was a light there was a light
               10. 10. 10. 10   79 sts.; Amen   Nicholas Breton
               1601 The Ravished Soul, pp. 13-27

98.   Before thy face, and in thy sight
               C. M.   9 sts.   William Hunnis
               1597 The Poore Widowes Mite, bound with Seven
               Sobs of a Sorrowful Soul for Sinne, pp. 34-
               35
               Tune in the same volume   William Hunnis

99.   **Behold a silly tender babe
               **C. M.   7 sts.   Robert Southwell
               **1634 St. Peter's Complaint etc., pp. 96-97
               1856 Reprint

100.   **Behold by misadventure, how the wind
               **14 decasyllables   Barnaby Barnes
               **1595 A Divine Centurie of Spirituall Sonnets
               1815 Reprint, p. 41

101.   **Behold, dear Father! with whose gracious eyes
               **14 decasyllables   Barnaby Barnes
               **1595 A Divine Centurie of Spirituall Sonnets
               1815 Reprint, p. 18

102.   Behold! he comes, comes from on high
               L. M.   7 sts.   Samuel Crossman
               1678 The Young Man's Divine Meditations in Some
               Sacred Poems, pp. 420-421

103.   Behold my right, and right my wrong
               8. 8. 8. 8. 8. 8   John Quarles
               1663 Divine Meditations... With... Divine Ejacula-
               tions, p. 132

104.   Behold, O God, the wretched state
               C. M. D.   5 sts.   William Hunnis

1597 Humble sutes of a sinner bound with <u>Com-</u>
<u>fortable Dialogs,</u> pp. 63-64
Tune in the same volume   William Hunnis

105.   Behold the great Creator makes
        See: Fairest of morning lights   Thomas Pestel

106.   Behold the King of Glory sits
        C. M.   5 sts.   Joseph Stennett
        1697 <u>Hys. in Commem.</u>, No. IV, p. 4
        No tune given but intended to be sung

107.   Behold, the sun that seem'd but now
        C. M. D.   3 sts.   George Wither
        1641 <u>Hal</u>. Pt. 1, No. XIV, pp. 20-21
        Suggested tune: <u>Psalm 16 or 18</u>

108.   Behold we come, dear Lord, to thee
        C. M.   7 sts.; Amen   John Austin
        1672 (1st ed. 1668) <u>Devotions</u>, No. 1, pp. 3-4
        1671 <u>Psalms and Hymns,</u> with
             tune, pp. 6-7   John Playford

109.   Betimes awake thee
        irreg.   14 sts.   Thomas Heywood
        1635 <u>The Hierarchie of the blessed Angells,</u>
             pp. 619-622

110.   Beware my heart
        4. 6. 4. 6. 4. 6. 4. 6. 8. 8   3 sts.   George Wither
        1641 <u>Hal</u>. Pt. 3, No. XLIII, pp. 441-442
        No tune given but intended to be sung

111.   Beware my heart, thou cherish not
        C. M. D.   3 sts.   George Wither
        1641 <u>Hal</u>. Pt. 1, No. LXXXIX, pp. 172-173
        Suggested tune: <u>Psalm 4</u>

112.   Bless me, Oh God! and be thou near
        10 octosyllables 4 sts.   George Wither
        1641 <u>Hal</u>. Pt. 1, No. XCVII, pp. 190-191
        No tune given but intended to be sung

113.   Blessed are the feet which bring the news
        See: Fair are the feet   John Mason

114.   Blessed be thy love
        See: Lord, now the time returns   John Austin

115.   **Blessed Creator! let thine only son
            **14 decasyllables   Barnaby Barnes
        **1595 A Divine Centurie of Spirituall Sonnets
            1815 Reprint, p. 3

116.   Blessed Lord, before you go
            irreg.   10 sts.   Lancelot Addison
        1699 Devotional Poems, pp. 21-23
        1754 C.H.C.G., Part I, No. 495, p. 290
            irreg.   29 ℓℓ.
        Tune to be selected by meter from appended
            Table of Metres and Tunes

117.   Blessed, O Lord, be thy wise grace
            C.M.   6 sts.; Amen   John Austin
        1672 (1st ed. 1668) Devotions, No. XII, p. 107
        1671 Psalms and Hymns, with
            tune, pp. 34-35   John Playford

118.   Blest angels, while we silent lie
            See: My God, now I from sleep   Thomas Ken
            awake

119.   Blest be my God that I was born
            C.M.D.   6 sts.   John Mason
        1683 Spiritual Songs, No. XV, pp. 34-36
            st. 6, ℓ. 5: "Glory to God the Father be"
        No tune given but intended to be sung

120.   Blest be the God of love
            6.10.8.8   8 sts.   George Herbert
        1633 The Temple, pp. 55-56
            st. 3, ℓ. 1: "My lord what have I brought
            thee home"
        1754 C.H.C.G., Pt. I, No. 366, p. 216
            L.M.   6 sts.
            Begins: "My Lord what have I brought thee
            home"
        Tune to be selected by meter from appended
            Table of Metres and Tunes

121.   Blest be thy love, dear Lord
            See: Lord, now the time returns   John Austin

122.   Blest day of God, most calm, most bright
            C.M.D.   6 sts.   John Mason
            C.M.   1 st.

1683 Spiritual Songs, No. XX, pp. 43-46
No tune given but intended to be sung

123.   Blest Father, Son, and Holy Ghost
          C. M. D.   8 sts.   George Wither
          1641 Hal. Pt. 1, No. XCV, pp. 185-187
          Suggested tune: Te Deum

124.   Blest Jesu! thou, on heaven intent
          See: My God, now I from sleep   Thomas Ken
          awake

125.   Blest little matyrs for the new-born God
          10.10.10.10   3 sts.   Lancelot Addison
          1699 Devotional Poems, pp. 38-39
          1754 C. H. C. G., Pt. I, No. 484, p. 281
          Tune to be selected by meter from appended
          Table of Metres and Tunes

126.   Blest Lord, I sigh and mourn, and come away
          irreg.   8 sts.   Lancelot Addison
          1699 Devotional Poems, pp. 6-8
          st. 2, ℓ. 1: "A bleeding heart I will present
          to thee"
          1754 C. H. C. G., Pt. I, No. 490, p. 288
          15 decasyllables
          Begins: "A bleeding heart I will present to
          thee"
          Tune to be selected by meter from appended
          Table of Metres and Tunes

127.   Blest spirits of the triumphant church above
          irreg.   5 sts.   Lancelot Addison
          1699 Devotional Poems, pp. 31-32

128.   Blest spirits, while you above shine bright and clear
          irreg.   12 sts.   Lancelot Addison
          1699 Devotional Poems, pp. 33-36
          1754 C. H. C. G., Pt. I, No. 514, p. 297
          Tune to be selected by meter from appended
          Table of Metres and Tunes

129.   Bright queen of heaven! God's virgin spouse
          C. M.   4 sts.   Henry Vaughan
          1655 Silex Scintillans, Pt. II, p. 35
        *1867 People's Hymnal, with tune, No. 193
          Begins: "Bright queen of saints"

130.   Bright queen of saints
               See: Bright queen of heaven   Henry Vaughan

131.   Bright shadows of true rest! some shoots of bliss
               10. 4. 10. 4. 10. 10. 10. 10   3 sts.   Henry Vaughan
               1650 Silex Scintillans, p. 68
                  From this: "Types of eternal rest, fair buds
                  of bliss"
               1852 Hys. for Christian Ch. and Hm., No. 636
               Choice of tunes from other books

132.   But art thou come, dear Saviour? hath thy love
               24 decasyllables   Sir Matthew Hale
               1676 Contemplations, "Poems upon Christmas-Day,"
                  No. XVI, (written in 1659) pp. 526-527
               1754 C. H. C. G., Pt. I, No. 414, pp. 236-237
               10. 10   12 sts.
               Tune to be selected by meter from appended
               Table of Metres and Tunes

133.   But man rebels, and for one tast doth choose
               See: Almighty God, when   Sir Matthew Hale
               he had raised

134.   But that I may on thee, O Lord
               C. M. D.   4 sts.   George Wither
               1641 Hal. Pt. 3, No. XVII, pp. 382-383
               Suggested tune: Psalm 4

135.   But that, no wonders, things appear
               C. M. D.   3 sts.   George Wither
               1641 Hal. Pt. 1, No. VII, pp. 10-11
               Suggested tune: Psalm 2, 6, or 7

136.   But that thou art my wisdome, Lord
               8. 6. 8. 6   5 sts.   George Herbert
               1633 The Temple, pp. 87-88
               1737 Collection of Psalms and Hymns, No. IX,
                  p. 47
               8. 8. 8. 8   4 sts.
               Begins: "Thou Lord my power and wisdom art"
               No tune given but intended to be sung

137.   By art, a poet is not made
               10 octosyllables 7 sts.   George Wither
               1641 Hal. Pt. 3, No. LX, pp. 478-480
               No tune given but intended to be sung

138.   By his endeavors no man may
           C. M. D.   5 sts.   George Wither
        1641 Hal. Pt. 1, No. CV, pp. 206-208
        Suggested tune: Psalm 4

139.   By his examples, teach us Lord
           L. M. D.   3 sts.   George Wither
        1641 Hal. Pt. 2, No. XLIIII
        Suggested tune: 10 Com.

140.   By me, or by my Father's house
           C. M. D.   8 sts.   George Wither
        1641 Hal. Pt. 3, No. II, pp. 352-354
        Suggested tune: Psalm 4

141.   By mercies and by judgements, Lord!
           C. M. D.   8 sts.   George Wither
        1641 Hal. Pt. 1, No. LXIX, pp. 127-130
        Suggested tune: Psalm 22

142.   By Thee were thy disciples taught
           L. M. D.   4 sts.   George Wither
        1641 Hal. Pt. 2, No. XLIX, pp. 320-321
        Suggested tune: Psalm 100

143.   By trusting unto thee, Oh God!
           L. M. D.   6 sts.   George Wither
        1641 Hal. Pt. 1, No. LXXI, pp. 131-133
        Suggested tune: Psalm 51

144. **By wand'ring I have lost myself
           **C. M.   12 sts.   Seventeenth Century
        1754 C. H. C. G., Pt. I, No. 504, pp. 293-294
        Tune to be selected by meter from appended
        Table of Metres and Tunes

145.   Can I not come to thee my God for these
           14 decasyllables   Robert Herrick
        1647 Noble Numbers, p. 16

146.   Canst be idle? canst thou play
           7. 7   George Herbert
           7. 7. 7   10 sts.
        1633 The Temple, pp. 105-106
        st. 1, ℓ. 3: "Rivers run, and springs each
           one"
        1754 C. H. C. G., Pt. I, No. 367, p. 216

7.7.7.7   6 sts.
Begins: "Rivers run, and springs each one"
Tune to be selected by meter from appended
    Table of Metres and Tunes

147.   Care for thy soul as thing of greatest price
            10.10.10.10.10.10   4 sts.
        1588 Psalms, Sonnets, and Songs, No. 31
            Tune in same volume   William Byrd

148.   Celestial virtue! Yet there are but few
            irreg.   9 sts.   Lancelot Addison
        1699 Devotional Poems, pp. 68-70
        st. 2, ℓ. 1: "If man think meanly (O my soul)
            of thee"

149.   Christ leads me through no darker room
            See: My whole though broken   Richard Baxter
                heart, O Lord

150.   Christ, when he died, deceiv'd the cross
            L.M.   3 sts.   Richard Crashaw
        1648 Steps to the Temple, pp. 14-15
        1754 C.H.C.G., Pt. I, No. 397, p. 230
            L.M.   4 sts.
        Tune to be selected by meter from appended
            Table of Metres and Tunes

151.   Christ who knows all his sheep
            See: My soul go boldly forth   Richard Baxter

152.   Close now thine eyes, and rest secure
            irreg.   10 ℓℓ.   Francis Quarles
        1632 Divine Fancies, Bk. IV, No. 2, p. 164
        1671 Psalms and Hymns, with
            tune, p. 91   John Playford
        Begins: "Close thine eyes and sleep secure"
        This hymn attributed to King Charles I in
            Miscellanae Sacra and Harmonia Sacra, Vol-
            ume 1.

153.   Come blessed spirit, descend and light on me
            irreg.   7 sts.   Lancelot Addison
        1699 Devotional Poems, pp. 26-28
        1754 C.H.C.G., Pt. I, No. 499, p. 291
            10.10.10.10   4 sts.
        Tune to be selected by meter from appended
            Table of Metres and Tunes

154.   Come bring thy gifts, if blessings were as slow
            10.10.10.10.10.10   4 sts.   George Herbert
            4.4.5.3.4.5   3 sts.
            1633 The Temple, pp. 141-142
            st. 4, ℓ. 1: "There is a balsam, or indeed a
                blood"
            1754 C.H.C.G., Pt. I, No. 354, p. 212
            Begins: "There is a balsam, or indeed a
                blood"
            Tune to be selected by meter from appended
                Table of Metres and Tunes

155.   Come, come, my dearest Lord
            See: I sojourn in a vale of tears   John Mason

156.   Come, dearest Lord and feed thy sheep
            See: My Lord, my love was   John Mason
                crucified

157.   Come, drop your branches, strow the way
            irreg.   10 sts.   Henry Vaughan
            1655 Silex Scintillans, Pt. II, pp. 27-28

158.   Come, H. Spirit, come and breath
            L.M.   7 sts.; Amen   John Austin
            1672 (1st ed. 1668) Devotions, No. XXXIII,
                pp. 290-291
            1671 Psalms and Hymns, with
                tune, p. 59   John Playford

159.   Come, H. Spirit, send down those beams
            8.8.6.8.8.6   John Austin
            1672 (1st ed. 1668) Devotions, No. XXXV,
                pp. 317-318
            1701 Devot. ed. H., p. 429; tune p. 10, separate
                section

160.   Come holy spirit the God of might
            C.M.D.   6 sts.   Unknown
        c.1559 The First Parte of the Booke of Psalmes,
                unpaged
            Tune in same volume   Unknown

161.   Come let's adore the gracious hand
            8.6.8.6   8 sts.; Amen   John Austin
            1672 (1st ed. 1668) Devotions, No. IX, pp. 80-
                81

1671 Psalms and Hymns, with
tune, pp. 80-81   John Playford

162.   Come, let's adore the king of love
        C. M.   7 sts.; Amen   John Austin
        1672 (1st ed. 1668) Devotions, No. XXII,
             pp. 178-179
        1701 Devot. ed. H., p. 234; tune p. 1, separate
        section

163.   Come let us all, who here have seen
        L. M.   9 sts.   Joseph Stennett
        1697 Hys. in Commem., No. XXXIV, p. 44
        Suggested tune: Psalm 100

164.   Come, let us praise our Master's hand
        C. M. D.   4 sts.   John Mason
        1683 Spiritual Songs, No. V, p. 14-15
        No tune given but intended to be sung

165.   Come, Lord, my head doth burn, my heart is sick
        10. 8. 10. 8. 6. 6   13 sts.   George Herbert
        1633 The Temple, pp. 99-101
        1754 C. H. C. G., Pt. I, No. 370, p. 217
        L. M. + refrain 8. 8   11 sts.
        Begins: "Faint is my head, and sick my
             heart"
        Tune to be selected by meter from appended
        Table of Metres and Tunes

166.   Come, Lord, when grace has made me meet
        See: My whole, though broken
             heart, O Lord   Richard Baxter

167.   Come mild and holy dove
        S. M.   10 sts.; Amen   John Austin
        1672 (1st ed. 1668) Devotions, No. XXXIV,
             pp. 308-309
        1701 Devot. ed. H., p. 415; tune p. 9, separate
        section

168.   Come my thoughts, that fondly fly
        7. 8. 7. 8   8 sts.; Amen   John Austin
        1672 (1st ed. 1668) Devotions, No. XX,
             pp. 175-176
        1701 Devot. ed. H., p. 230; tune p. 8, separate
        section

169.   Come, my way, my truth, my life
            7.7.7.7   3 sts.   George Herbert
        1633 The Temple, p. 150
        1754 C.H.C.G., Pt. I, No. 376, p. 219
            7.7.7.7   3 sts.
        Tune to be selected by meter from appended
            Table of Metres and Tunes

170.   Come, ravisht soul with high delight
        *1659 Sermons and Devotions Old   Thomas Pestel
            and New
        st. 2, ℓ. 1: "O sing the glories"
        *1894 Hymns Supplemental, Horder, with tune, No.
            1016
        Begins: "O sing the glories"

171.   Come to me God; but do not come
            16 octosyllables   Robert Herrick
        1647 Noble Numbers, p. 67

172.   **Come to your heaven, you heavenly choirs
            **8.8.8.8.8.8   8 sts.   Robert Southwell
        **1634 St. Peter's Complaint etc.
        1856 Reprint, pp. 100-102

173.   Come ye hither, all whose taste
            7.3.7.7.3.7   6 sts.   George Herbert
        1633 The Temple, pp. 174-175
        1754 C.H.C.G., Pt. I, No. 377, p. 219
            6.6.7.7.7.7   4 sts.
        Begins: "Look hither, ye whose taste"
        Tune to be selected by meter from appended
            Table of Metres and Tunes

174.   Confession of the same I owe
            C.M.D.   7 sts.   George Wither
        1641 Hal. Pt. 3, No. XXII, pp. 394-396
        Suggested tune: Psalm 1

175.   **Content thyself with patience
            **8 octosyllables   [Robert Smith]
        1754 C.H.C.G., Pt. I, No. 352, p. 212
        Tune to be selected by meter from appended
            Table of Metres and Tunes

176.   Dear beauteous death! the jewel of the just
            See: They are all gone into   Henry Vaughan
            the world of light

177.   **Dear Comforter with whose dear precious blood
              **14 decasyllables   Barnaby Barnes
           **1595 A Divine Centurie of Spirituall Sonnets
           1815 Reprint, p. 3

178.   **Dear Dove, thy pris'ner may I be
              **L. M.   12 sts.   [Faithfull Teate]
           1754 C. H. C. G. , Pt. I, No. 390, pp. 227-228
           Tune to be selected by meter from appended
           Table of Metres and Tunes

179.   Dear God! how great, how large a grace
              L. M. D.   4 sts.   George Wither
           1641 Hal. Pt. 1, No. XLVIII, pp. 79-80
           No tune given but intended to be sung

180.   Dear God! that watch dost keep
              S. M. D.   4 sts.   George Wither
           1641 Hal. Pt. 1, No. II, pp. 3-4
           Suggested tune: Psalm 25 or 67

181.   Dear God, the Pharoah of our Souls
              8. 8. 8. 8. 8. 8   John Quarles
           1663 Divine Meditations... With... Divine Ejacula-
                tions, p. 160

182.   Dear Jesu, when, when will it be
              L. M.   12 sts.; Amen   John Austin
           1672 (1st ed. 1668) Devotions, No. IV, pp. 40-
                42
           1701 Devot. ed. H., p. 49; tune p. 2, separate
                section

183.   Dear mystery, dear Lord, dear great Three-one
              irreg.   9 sts.   Lancelot Addison
           1699 Devotional Poems, pp. 28-31
           1754 C. H. C. G., Pt. I, No. 501, p. 293
           10. 10. 10. 10   7 sts.
           Tune to be selected by meter from appended
           Table of Metres and Tunes

184.   Dear Saviour, Oh! what ails this heart
              14 octosyllables 3 sts.
           1696 Nahum Tate Miscellanae Sacra, Vol. I, pp.
                18-20
           1701 Divine Companion, with tune,   Mr. Akeroyd
                p. 36

185.   Dearest, ascending Lord, before we part
            irreg.   3 sts.   Lancelot Addison
        1699 Devotional Poems, pp. 15-16

186.   Dearest master, must we part
            irreg.   3 sts.   Lancelot Addison
        1699 Devotional Poems, pp. 16-17

187.   Death and darkness get you packing
            18 octosyllables   Henry Vaughan
        1650 Silex Scintillans, p. 80

188.   Death steals upon us unawares
            C. M. D.   4 sts.   [Thomas Shepherd]
            C. M.   1 st.
        1693 Penetential Cries, No. XXXI, p. 46
        No tune given but intended to be sung

189.   Death, the old serpent's son
            irreg.   19 ℓℓ.; Amen   Jeremy Taylor
        1655 Festival Hymns appended to The Golden
            Grove, pp. 154-155
        ℓ. 2: "Thou hads't a sting once like thy sire"
        1754 C. H. C. G., Pt. I, No. 408, p. 233
            C. M.   4 sts.
        Begins: "He had a sting once like his sire"
        Tune to be selected by meter from appended
            Table of Metres and Tunes

190.   Descend, O King of Saints, descend
            L. M.   8 sts.   Joseph Stennett
        1697 Hys. in Commem., No. IV, p. 4
        Suggested tune: Psalm 100

191.   Descend to thy Jerusalem, O Lord
            See: Lord, come away   Jeremy Taylor

192.   Direct my steps, Lord, be my way
            8. 8. 8. 8. 8. 8   John Quarles
        1663 Divine Meditations... With... Divine Ejacula-
            tions, p. 175

193.   Direct, O God, the judge's breast
            8. 8. 8. 8. 8. 8   John Quarles
        1663 Divine Meditations... With... Divine Ejacula-
            tions, p. 152

194.   Discourage not thyself my soul
        L. M. D.   6 sts.   George Wither
        1641 Hal. Pt. 3, No. IX, pp. 366-368
        Suggested tune: Psalm 100

195.   Do I resolve any easy life
        8. 7. 7. 7   8 sts.; Amen   John Austin
        1672 (1st ed. 1668) Devotions, No. XIX, pp. 169-
        170
        1701 Devot. ed. H., p. 222; tune p. 7, separate
        section

196.   Draw nigh to thy Jerusalem
        See: Lord, come away   Jeremy Taylor

197.   Drop, drop, slow tears
        4. 6   12 ℓ ℓ .   Phineas Fletcher
        1633 Poeticall Miscellanies appended to The Pur-
        ple Isle, p. 96
        1852 Hys. for Christian Ch. and Hm., 9th ed.,
        No. 415
        Choice of tunes from other books

198.   Due fear, becomes us well
        S. M. D.   4 sts.   George Wither
        1641 Hal. Pt. 1, No. XC, pp. 173-174
        Suggested tune: Psalm 25

199.   Earth's but a sorry tent
        See: Sweet place, sweet   Samuel Crossman
        place alone

200.   Enrich, Lord, heart, mouth, hands in me
        See: Lord, who hast formed   George Herbert
        me out of mud

201.   Eternal Father, how divine
        L. M.   8 sts.   Joseph Stennett
        1697 Hys. in Commem., No. XXIX, p. 37
        Suggested tune: Psalm 100

202.   Eternal God, before whose eyes
        8. 8. 8. 8. 8. 8   John Quarles
        1663 Divine Meditations... With... Divine Ejacula-
        tions, p. 155

203.   Eternal God, whose name is love

       L. M. D.   6 sts.   Richard Baxter
    1681 Poetical Fragments, pp. 75-76
    Suggested tune: Psalm 51

204.   Eternal Maker, grant that we
       8. 8. 8. 8. 8. 8   John Quarles
    1663 Divine Meditations... With... Divine Ejacula-
       tions, p. 158

205.   Eternal mover; whose diffused glory
       11. 10. 11. 10. 10. 10   6 sts.   Sir Henry Wotton
    1651 Reliquiae Wottonianae, pp. 529-530

206.   Evening Hymn
       See: All praise to thee, my   Thomas Ken
       God this night

207.   Exceeding faithful to thy word
       C. M. D.   6 sts.   George Wither
    1623 Hymns and Songs, No. LVIII
    Tune in same volume:
       Song 3   Orlando Gibbons

208.   Exceeding gracious favours, Lord
       8. 8. 8. 8. 8. 8   4 sts.   George Wither
    1623 Hymns and Songs, No. LXXIV
    Tune in same volume:
       Song 9   Orlando Gibbons

209.   Except, when kindest we appear
       C. M. D.   8 sts.   George Wither
    1641 Hal. Pt. 3, No. XXIII, pp. 396-398
    Suggested tune: Psalm 1

210.   Experiment, I now have had
       C. M. D.   5 sts.   George Wither
    1641 Hal. Pt. 1, No. CX, pp. 216-217
    Suggested tune: Te Deum

211.   Fain would I view that pleasing sight
       10 octosyllables 5 sts.   George Wither
    1641 Hal. Pt. 3, No. XLVII, pp. 449-451
    Suggested tune: Lamentation

212.   Fain would my thoughts fly up to Thee
       C. M.   9 sts.; Amen   John Austin
    1672 (1st ed. 1668) Devotions, No. XI, pp. 102-
       103

1671 Psalms and Hymns, with
    tune, pp. 84-85   John Playford

213.   **Faind Janus now forget thy name
         **8. 8. 8. 8. 10. 10   4 sts.   Joseph Beaumont
     **c.1643 Minor Poems, MS.
        **Marked: To a Base & 2 Trebles
     1914 Reprint, p. 157

214.   Faint is my head, and sick my heart
         See: Come, Lord, my head   George Herbert
         doth burn

215.   Fair are the feet which bring the news
         C. M. D.   5 sts.   John Mason
     1683 Spiritual Songs, No. XVI, pp. 36-38
     No tune given but intended to be sung
     1841 Christian Psalmody, No. 429
       Begins: "Bless'd are the feet which bring the
       news"
     Suggested tune: Any C. M. tune

216.   **Fairest of morning lights appear
         **C. M.   7 sts.   Thomas Pestel
     **1659 Sermons and Devotions
       st. 5, ℓ. 1: "Behold the great creator makes"
     1890 Palgrave, p. 69
     1906 The English Hymnal,
       with tune, No. 20   Ancient English Carol
       Begins: "Behold the great creator makes"

217.   Farewell, dear Lord, I kiss your sacred feet
         See: Adieu, dear Lord, I   Lancelot Addison
         kiss your sacred feet

218.   Farewell, dear Master, we must part I see
         See: Adieu, dear Master,   Lancelot Addison
         we must part I see

219.   Farewell, dear Saviour, till we meet above
         irreg.   3 sts.   Lancelot Addison
     1699 Devotional Poems, pp. 17-18

220.   Farewell poor world! I must be gone
         L. M.   7 sts.   Samuel Crossman
     1678 The Young Man's Divine Meditations in Some
       Sacred Poems

*1884 The Comprehensive Rippon

221.   Farewell, vain world, I bid adieu
            C. M. D.   4 sts.   [Thomas Shepherd]
            1693 Penetential Cries, No. VIII, p. 15
            No tune given but intended to be sung

222.   **Father divine, before thy view
            C. M.   4 sts.   [Jeremy] Taylor
            1839 Hendie, No. 138
            No tune given but intended to be sung

223.   Father if justly still we claim
            See: When Christ His body up   Henry More
                    had borne

224.   Father of heaven, and Him, by whom
            8.10.10.10.8.6.10.10.10   28 sts.   John Donne
            1633 Poems by J. D., pp. 172-185
            1754 C. H. C. G., Pt. I, No. 384, p. 224
            10.10.10.10   6 sts.
            Tune to be selected by meter from appended
            Table of Metres and Tunes

225.   **Father of our feeble race
            7.7.7.7.7.7.7.7   3 sts.   [Jeremy] Taylor
            1839 Hendie, No. 344
            No tune given but intended to be sung

226.   Feigned Janus, now forget thy name
            See: Faind Janus, now   Joseph Beaumont
                    forget thy name

227.   **Firm rock of during stone, sure bulwark of defense
            **14 decasyllables   Barnaby Barnes
            **1595 A Divine Centurie of Spirituall Sonnets
            1815 Reprint, p. 32

228.   **For comfort, my dear God! I did attend
            **14 decasyllables   Barnaby Barnes
            **1595 A Divine Centurie of Spirituall Sonnets
            1815 Reprint, p. 32

229.   For spreading Lord, our table, thus
            C. M. D.   2 sts.   George Wither
            1641 Hal. Pt. 1, No. XXXIV, p. 56
            Suggested tune: Magnificat

230.   For those blest penmen of thy word
         L. M. D.   3 sts.   George Wither
         1623 Hymns and Songs, No. LXVIII, p. 49
         Tune in same volume:
            Song 44   Orlando Gibbons

231.   Forbear to shed excessive tears
         L. M. D.   4 sts.   George Wither
         1641 Hal. Pt. 1, No. LXXXV, pp. 160-161
         Suggested tune: 10 Com.

232.   Foul-Spirits may, our hearts possess
         C. M. D.   8 sts.   George Wither
         1641 Hal. Pt. 2, No. IX, pp. 241-243
         Suggested tune: Psalm 4

233.   **Fountain of life and endless happiness
            **14 decasyllables   Barnaby Barnes
        **1595 A Divine Centurie of Spirituall Sonnets
         1815 Reprint, p. 12.

234.   Fountain of light, and living breath
            8. 8. 8. 8. 8. 8   John Quarles
         1663 Divine Meditations... With... Divine Ejacula-
            tions, p. 139
         1852 Hys. for Christian Ch. and Hm., 9th ed.,
            No. 440
         Choice of tunes from other books

235.   **Fountain of sweets, eternal dove
            **8 octosyllables; Hallelujah   Joseph Beaumont
        **c.1643 Minor Poems, MS.
            **Marked: To a Base & 2 Trebles
         1914 Reprint, p. 195

236.   From colds late nipping herbs and trees
         C. M. D.   2 sts.   George Wither
         1641 Hal. Pt. 1, No. LXVIII, p. 127
         Suggested tune: Te Deum

237.   From supper to Gethsemane
         C. M.   10 sts.   Joseph Stennett
         1697 Hys. in Commem., No. XXI, p. 26
         No tune given but intended to be sung

238.   *From the deeps of grief and fear
          *1663 Poetical Miscellanies,   Phineas Fletcher
                p. 63

*1887 Congregational Church Hymnal

239.   **Full of celestial syrups, full or sweet
        **14 decasyllables   Barnaby Barnes
        **1595 A Divine Centurie of Spirituall Sonnets
        1815 Reprint, p. 27

240.   Full of mercy, full of love
            irreg.   20 ℓℓ.; Amen   Jeremy Taylor
        1655 Festival and Penetentiall Hymns appended to
            The Golden Grove, pp. 168-169
        ℓ. 3: "Thou who taught the blind man's night"
        1754 C.H.C.G., Pt. I, No. 406, p. 232
        L.M.   4 sts.
        Begins: "O thou who taught at the blind man's
            night"
        Tune to be selected by meter from appended
            Table of Metres and Tunes

241.   Full of wrath, his threatning breath
            irreg. (18 ℓℓ.; Allelujah; Amen) Jeremy Taylor
        1655 Festival Hymnes, appended to The Golden
            Grove, pp. 159-160

242.   Full well, that person, it beseems
            L.M.D.   6 sts.   George Wither
        1641 Hal. Pt. 3, No. IIII, pp. 356-358
        Suggested tune: 10 Com.

243.   Give ear, O Lord, to hear
            S.M.D.   3 sts.; Amen   William Hunnis
        1597 Humble Sutes of a Sinner bound with Com-
            fortable Dialogs, pp. 61-62
        Tune in same volume   William Hunnis

244.   Give me my captive soul
            See: Not in rich furniture,   George Herbert
                or fine array

245.   Give me the heart, O God to trust
            8.8.8.8.8.8   John Quarles
        1663 Divine Meditations... With... Divine Ejacula-
            tions, p. 166

246.   Glorious Creator, once more thine
            8.8.8.8.8.8   John Quarles
        1663 Divine Meditations... With... Divine Ejacula-
            tions, p. 152

247.   Glory to God on high
            S. M.   10 sts.   Joseph Stennett
        1697 Hym. in Commem., No. XX, p. 24

248.   *Glory to God the Father be
            See: Blest be my God that I   John Mason
            was born

249.   *Glory to thee in light arrayed
            See: My God, now I from sleep   Thomas Ken
            awake

250.   *Glory to thee, my God, this night
            See: All praise to thee my God,   Thomas Ken
            this night

251.   *Glory to thee who safe hast kept
            See: Awake my soul, and with   Thomas Ken
            the sun

252.   God is ascended up on high
            L. M.   12 sts.   Henry More
        1668 Divine Hymns appended to Divine Dialogues,
            pp. 502-504
        1920 The Oxford Hymn Book,
            with tune, No. 112   George Frederick Handel

253.   God who once more unseal'd mine eyes
            L. M.   7 sts.   [Thomas Shepherd]
        1693 Penetential Cries, No. XIX, p. 30
        Suggested tune: Psalm 100

254.   God's furnace doth in Sion stand
            See: I that am drawn out of the   John Mason
            depth

255.   Good God! thy mercy and thy might
            8. 8. 8. 8. 8. 8   John Quarles
        1663 Divine Meditations... With... Divine Ejacula-
            tions, p. 164

256.   Good God, where ere I cast mine eyes
            8. 8. 8. 8. 8. 8   John Quarles
        1663 Divine Meditations... With... Divine Ejacula-
            tions, p. 170

257.   *Gracious redeemer, how divine

C. M. 7 sts. Joseph Stennett
1697 Hys. in Commem., No. XII, p. 14
No tune given but intended to be sung

258. Great almighty King of Heaven
7.7.7.7.7.7 8 sts. George Wither
1641 Hal. Pt. 3, No. LXII, pp. 484-486
No tune given but intended to be sung

259. Great bridegroom, fill thy dearest spouse
8. 8. 8. 8. 8. 8 John Quarles
1663 Divine Meditations... With... Divine Ejaculations, p. 142

260. Great God, and just! how canst thou see
irreg. 27 ℓ ℓ.; Amen Jeremy Taylor
1655 Festival and Penetential Hymns appended
to The Golden Grove, pp. 167-168
1688 Harmonia Sacra, with tune,
pp. 58-60 Henry Purcell

261. Great God, my strength, at whose command
8. 8. 8. 8. 8. 8 John Quarles
1663 Divine Meditations... With... Divine Ejaculations, p. 133

262. **Great God of Abraham! whose eternal power
**14 decasyllables Barnaby Barnes
**1595 A Divine Centurie of Spirituall Sonnets
1815 Reprint, p. 11

263. Great God of gods, great King of kings
8. 8. 8. 8. 8. 8 John Quarles
1663 Divine Meditations... With... Divine Ejaculations, p. 157

264. Great God of wonders, that dost ope
8. 8. 8. 8. 8. 8 John Quarles
1663 Divine Meditations... With... Divine Ejaculations, p. 158

265. Great God, the work of whose high hands
8. 8. 8. 8. 8. 8 John Quarles
1663 Divine Meditations... With... Divine Ejaculations, p. 133

266. Great God thou art a God of grace
C. M. D. 6 sts. [Thomas Shepherd]

1693 Penetential Cries, No. X, p. 17
   st. 3, ℓℓ. 1-4 the same as last four lines of
   "O Lord turn not thy face away"
   st. 6, ℓℓ. 5-8 repeat them.
   No tune given but intended to be sung

267.   Great God, thy garden is defaced
          8. 8. 8. 8. 8. 8   John Quarles
          1663 Divine Meditations... With... Divine Ejacula-
          tions, p. 130

268.   Great God to whom all praise belongs
          8. 8. 8. 8. 8. 8   John Quarles
          1663 Divine Meditations... With... Divine Ejacula-
          tions, p. 174

269.   Great God, who dost the world command
          C. M. D.   4 sts.   John Mason
          1683 Spiritual Songs, No. XXVII, pp. 58-59
          No tune given but intended to be sung

270.   Great God, whom fools deny, how dare
          8. 8. 8. 8. 8. 8   John Quarles
          1663 Divine Meditations... With... Divine Ejacula-
          tions, p. 131

271.   Great God, whose ever-wakefull eye
          8. 8. 8. 8. 8. 8   John Quarles
          1663 Divine Meditations... With... Divine Ejacula-
          tions, p. 165

272.   Great God whose goodness doth repleate
          8. 8. 8. 8. 8. 8   John Quarles
          1663 Divine Meditations... With... Divine Ejacula-
          tions, p. 173

273.   Great God whose kingdom hath no end
          8. 8. 8. 8. 8. 8   John Quarles
          1663 Divine Meditations... With... Divine Ejacula-
          tions, p. 173

274.   Great God, whose promise is to hear
          8. 8. 8. 8. 8. 8   John Quarles
          1663 Divine Meditations... With... Divine Ejacula-
          tions, p. 158

275.   Great God, whose scepter rules the earth
          8. 8. 8. 8. 8. 8   John Quarles

1663 Divine Meditations... With... Divine Ejaculations, p. 127

276.   Great judge of all, how we vile wretches quake
        irreg.   32 ℓ ℓ .; Amen   Jeremy Taylor
        1655 Festival Hymns appended to The Golden
        Grove, pp. 156-157

277.   Great king of glory, who are dressed
        8. 8. 8. 8. 8. 8   John Quarles
        1663 Divine Meditations... With... Divine Ejacula-
        tions, p. 157

278.   Great king of peace, be pleased to send
        8. 8. 8. 8. 8. 8   John Quarles
        1663 Divine Meditations... With... Divine Ejacula-
        tions, p. 176

279.   Great Lord of time! great king of heav'n
        L. M. D.   7 sts.   George Wither
        1641 Hal. Pt. 2, No. II, pp. 229-231
        Suggested tune: Psalm 100

280.   Great Lord of wonders, thou by whom
        8. 8. 8. 8. 8. 8   John Quarles
        1663 Divine Meditations... With... Divine Ejacula-
        tions, p. 138

281.   Great monarch of the world, disclose
        8. 8. 8. 8. 8. 8   John Quarles
        1663 Divine Meditations... With... Divine Ejacula-
        tions, p. 156

282.   Great (Oh Lord) thy favour was
        7. 7. 7. 7. 7. 7. 7. 7   6 sts.   George Wither
        1641 Hal. Pt. 3, No. XXIIII, pp. 399-400
        No tune given but intended to be sung

283.   Great prince of peace, whose kingdom brings
        8. 8. 8. 8. 8. 8   John Quarles
        1663 Divine Meditations... With... Divine Ejacula-
        tions, p. 150

284.   Great shepherd of my soul, thy hand
        8. 8. 8. 8. 8. 8   John Quarles
        1663 Divine Meditations... With... Divine Ejacula-
        tions, p. 134

285.   Great son of the eternal God
             8. 8. 8. 8. 8. 8   John Quarles
             1663 Divine Meditations... With... Divine Ejacula-
                 tions, p. 128

286.   Great spring, from whence all mercy flows
             8. 8. 8. 8. 8. 8   John Quarles
             1663 Divine Meditations... With... Divine Ejacula-
                 tions, p. 154

287.   Great without controversy great
             L. M.   8 sts.   [Christopher Harvey]
             1673 The Synagogue, pp. 39-40
             1754 C. H. C. G., Pt. I, No. 380, p. 221
             Tune to be selected by meter from appended
             Table of Metres and Tunes

288.   Had not, Oh Lord, thy grace
             S. M. D.   5 sts.   George Wither
             1641 Hal. Pt. 1, No. C, pp. 196-197
             Suggested tune: Psalm 25

289.   Hail, holy Lord! I bow and joy to see
             irreg.   6 sts.   Lancelot Addison
             1699 Devotional Poems, pp. 9-10
             1754 C. H. C. G., Pt. I, No. 492, p. 289
             10. 10. 10. 10   5 sts.
             Tune to be selected by meter from appended
             Table of Metres and Tunes

290.   *Hallelujah: Hark how ye joyfull heavns rebound
             **4. 8. 8. 4. 2. 2. 6. 8   7 sts.   Joseph Beaumont
         **c.1643 Minor Poems, MS.
             **Marked: The Hymn Sett to 5 parts for voices
                 and Violls, by R. C.
             1914 Reprint, pp. 191-192

291.   Hallelujah, now I sing
             10 septisyllables   11 sts.   George Wither
             2 septisyllables   Chorus
             1641 Hal. Pt. 3, No. I, pp. 347-351
             No tune given but intended to be sung

292.   Happy are they our Lord was chose
             C. M.   9 sts.   Joseph Stennett
             1697 Hys. in Commem., No. XXXV, p. 46
             No tune given but intended to be sung

293.   Hark, my soul, how everything
              7. 7. 7. 7   8 sts.; Amen   John Austin
        1672 (1st ed. 1668) Devotions, No. VI, pp. 65-66
        1701 Devot. ed. H., p. 79; tune p. 11, separate
              section

294.   Hast not heard, that my Lord Jesus dy'd
              See: Away despair; my gra-   George Herbert
              cious Lord doth hear

295.   Hast thou, my soul, thy Saviour view'd
              L. M.   8 sts.   Joseph Stennett
        1697 Hys. in Commem., No. XXVI, p. 33
        Suggested tune: Psalm 100

296.   Have, have ye no regard, all ye
              8. 8. 8   5 sts.   Robert Herrick
        1647 Noble Numbers, p. 75

297.   He had a sting once like his sire
              See: Death the old serpent's   Jeremy Taylor
              son

298.   He is risen higher, not set
              irreg.   10 ℓ ℓ.; Amen   Jeremy Taylor
        1655 Festival Hymns appended to The Golden
              Grove, p. 165

299.   He that a voyage undertakes
              8. 8. 6. 8. D.   11 sts.   George Wither
        1641 Hal. Pt. 1, No. XXIII, pp. 34-37
        Suggested tune: Psalm 4

300.   He that can in a moment space
              C. M. D.   7 sts.   George Wither
        1641 Hal. Pt. 2, No. VIII, pp. 238-241
        Suggested tune: Psalm 4

301.   He that his Father had forsook
              L. M. D.   4 sts.   George Wither
        1623 Hymns and Songs, No. LXXIII, p. 51
        Tune in same volume: Song 44
                                              Orlando Gibbons

302.   **He that his mirth hath lost
              **S. M.   38 sts.   Robert Southwell
        **1634 Saint Peter's Complaint, pp. 81-87

1856 Reprint
st. 27, ℓ. 1: "Yet God's I must remain"

303.   He that is down needs fear no fall
         C. M.   3 sts.   John Bunyan
         1744 (1st ed. 1684) Pilgrim's Progress, Pt. II,
         p. 85
         1931 Songs of Praise, with
         tune, No. 513   Samuel Stanley

304.   *He wants not friends that hath thy love
         See: Lord, I have cast up   Richard Baxter
         the account

305.   He who would valiant be
         See: Who would true valour see   John Bunyan

306.   Health is a jewel dropt from heav'n
         C. M. D.   4 sts.   John Mason
         1683 Spiritual Songs, No. VII, pp. 17-19
         No tune given but intended to be sung

307.   Hear me, my God, when I to thee
         C. M.   9 sts.
         1701 Divine Companion, with tune,
         p. 44   William Croft

308.   Hear me, O god!
         4. 4. 4. 4   6 sts.   Ben. Johnson [sic]
         1640 Underwoods, p. 164
         *1882 The Church of England Hymn Book, ed.
         Godfrey Thring

309.   Hear! Oh great almighty King
         12 septisyllables   8 sts.   George Wither
         1641 Hal. Pt. 1, No. LXIII, pp. 118-121
         No tune given but intended to be sung

310.   Hearer of prayers, confound my foes
         8. 8. 8. 8. 8. 8   John Quarles
         1663 Divine Meditations... With... Divine Ejacula-
         tions, p. 145

311.   Hearer of prayers, to whom should I
         8. 8. 8. 8. 8. 8   John Quarles
         1663 Divine Meditations... With... Divine Ejacula-
         tions, p. 168

312. *Her virgin eyes saw God incarnate born
          *cento from Sion: or, Philothea   Thomas Ken
       *1721 Works, vol. IV, p. 370
          **When she to Bethlehem came that happy
             morn"
       1906 The English Hymnal with Tunes,
             No. 217   H. Lawes
          **10.10.10.10

313. Here a little child I stand
          7.7.7.7.7.7   with Amen   Robert Herrick
       1647 Noble Numbers, p. 31
       1931 Songs of Praise, with tune,
             No. 402   Geoffrey Shaw

314. Here, dear Lord, I love to be
          irreg.   6 sts.   Lancelot Addison
       1699 Devotional Poems, pp. 46-47
       1754 C.H.C.G., Pt. I, No. 525, p. 300
       Tune to be selected by meter from appended
       Table of Metres and Tunes

315. Here I converse can freely with my love
          8 decasyllables   Lancelot Addison
       1699 Devotional Poems, p. 51
       1754 C.H.C.G., Pt. I, No. 524, p. 200
       Tune to be selected by meter from appended
       Table of Metres and Tunes

316. Here let me sigh, and sighing see
          See: And art thou come,   Lancelot Addison
          blest Babe, and come to me

317. He's come, let every knee be bent
          C.M.   8 sts.
       1715 Divine Companion, with
             tune, p. 22   Jer. Clarke

318. *High praises meet and dwell within
          *1732 Multum in Parvo: or the   John Mason
             Jubilee of Jubilees

319. **High priest of Sion! whose eternal throne
          **14 decasyllables   Barnaby Barnes
          **1595 A Divine Centurie of Spirituall Sonnets
       1815 Reprint, p. 10

320. Highest of highest, that dost raise

8. 8. 8. 8. 8. 8   John Quarles
1663 Divine Meditations... With... Divine Ejaculations, p. 162

321.   Horrid darkness, sad and sore
              irreg.   26 ℓ ℓ .; Amen   Jeremy Taylor
        1655 Festival Hymnes appended to The Golden
              Grove, pp. 158-159

322.   How are Oh God! we sinners bound
              C. M. D.   6 sts.   George Wither
        1641 Hal. Pt. 1, No. XXIX, pp. 47-49
        Suggested tune: Psalm 4

323.   How beautiful the feet that bring
              See: Fair are the feet which   John Mason
                    bring the news

324.   How blest are we! who may repair
              C. M. D.   4 sts.   George Wither
        1641 Hal. Pt. 1, No. XXXVI, pp. 58-59
        Suggested tune: Psalm 117

325.   How blest the feet that bring the news
              See: Fair are the feet   John Mason

326.   How do I use my paper, ink and pen
              10.10.10.10.10.10   3 sts.   Henry Walpole
        1588 Psalmes, Sonets and Songs of Sadness,
              No. 33
        Tune in same volume   William Byrd

327.   How great! how gracious have I found
              L. M. D.   5 sts.   George Wither
        1641 Hal. Pt. 1, No. XXIII, pp. 38-39
        Suggested tune: Psalm 100

328.   How happy is he born and taught
              L. M.   6 sts.   Sir Henry Wotton
        1651 Reliquiae Wottonianae, pp. 522-523
        1827 A Collection of Psalms and Hymns, No. 210
        Suggested tune: Any L. M. tune

329.   How happy is it, and how sweet
              C. M. D.   7 sts.   George Wither
        1641 Hal. Pt. 1, No. XXXVIII, pp. 60-62
        Suggested tune: Psalm 133

330.   How hard is it for flesh and blood
         C. M. D.   7 sts.   George Wither
         1641 Hal. Pt. 1, No. LXXXI, pp. 153-155
         Suggested tune: Psalm 4

331.   How little did I hear, read, pray
             irreg.   7 sts.   Lancelot Addison
         1699 Devotional Poems, pp. 48-49
         1754 C. H. C. G., Pt. I, No. 527, p. 301
         L. M.   3 sts.
         Tune to be selected by meter from appended
             Table of Metres and Tunes

332.   How many Lord! how foul! how great
         C. M. D.   9 sts.   George Wither
         1641 Hal. Pt. 1, No. XCIIII, pp. 182-183
         Suggested tune: Psalm 22

333.   How many miracles of love
         C. M.   7 sts.   Joseph Stennett
         1697 Hys. in Commem., No. XV, p. 18
         No tune given but intended to be sung

334.   How near me, came the hand of death
         L. M. D.   6 sts.   George Wither
         1641 Hal. Pt. 3, No. XXVII, pp. 406-408
         Suggested tune: I loved thee once

335.   How oft, and by how many crimes
         C. M. D.   3 sts.   George Wither
         1623 Hymns and Songs, No. LXXXVI, p. 60
         Tune in same volume: Song 3 Orlando Gibbons

336.   How shall I sing that majesty
         C. M. D.   12 sts.   John Mason
         1683 Spiritual Songs, Song I, pp. 1-6
         st. 1, ℓ. 5: "Thousands of thousands stand
             around"
         No tune given but intended to be sung

337.   How sweet, how beauteous is the place
         C. M.   6 sts.   Joseph Stennett
         1697 Hys. in Commem., No. XVI, p. 19
         No tune given but intended to be sung

338.   How swiftly wafted in a sigh
             See: Whither, O whither art   George Herbert
             thou fled

339.   How uneasie are we here
            7. 7. 7. 7   6 sts.
        1701 Divine Companion, with tune,
            p. 31   Jer. Clarke

340.   **How uneasy does it seem
            **7. 7. 7. 7   3 sts.   Seventeenth Century
        1754 C. H. C. G., Pt. I, No. 528, p. 301
            Tune to be selected by meter from appended
            Table of Metres and Tunes

341.   How watchfull need we to become
            C. M. D.   4 sts.   George Wither
        1623 Hymns and Songs, No. LXXII, p. 51
            Tune in same volume: Song 3   Orlando Gibbons

342.   **How wrapt am I, how full of bliss
            **C. M.   23 sts.   [Sixteenth Century]
        1754 C. H. C. G., Pt. I, No. 422, pp. 241-242
            Tune to be selected by meter from appended
            Table of Metres and Tunes

343.   I am a tree that God has set
            C. M. D.   4 sts.   [Thomas Shepherd]
        1693 Penetential Cries, No. XXI, p. 32
            No tune given but intended to be sung

344.   I am afraid my God hath me forsook
            10. 10. 10. 10. 10   16 ℓℓ.   Benjamin Keach
        1681 Sion in Distress, 2nd ed., p. 77

345.   **I am the door, said Christ: the spear's sad art
            10. 10   [Richard Crashaw]
        1754 C. H. C. G., Pt. I, No. 394, p. 229
            Tune to be selected by meter from appended
            Table of Metres and Tunes

346.   I bless my God for giving grace
            C. M. D.   3 sts.   [Thomas Shepherd]
        1693 Penetential Cries, No. XIV, p. 24
            No tune given but intended to be sung

347.   I bow, blest Trinity, and in thee believe
            10. 10. 10   1 st.   Lancelot Addison
            10. 10. 10. 10   4 sts.
        1699 Devotional Poems, pp. 51-53
        1754 C. H. C. G., Pt. I, No. 502, pp. 292-293

Tune to be selected by meter from appended
Table of Metres and Tunes

348. I cannot ope mine eyes
          6. 8. 8. 10   5 sts.   George Herbert
          1633 The Temple, p. 54
          1754 C. H. C. G., Pt. I, No. 364, p. 215
          L. M.   5 sts.
          Begins: "I can't so much as ope my eyes"
          Tune to be selected by meter from appended
          Table of Metres and Tunes

349. I can't so much as ope my eyes
          See: I cannot ope mine eyes   George Herbert

350. **I feel, by motions in my sinnfull breast
          **14 decasyllables   Barnaby Barnes
          **1595 A Divine Centurie of Spirituall Sonnets
          1815 Reprint, p. 45

351. I got me flowers to straw thy way
          See: Rise heart, thy Lord is   George Herbert
          risen

352. I had a Lord, but ah he's gone
          L. M.   6 sts.   Thomas Shepherd
          1743 Spiritual Songs, (16th ed.) No. XXXII
          No tune given but intended to be sung

353. *I had one only thing to do
          *1721 Hymns for all the Festivals   Thomas Ken
          of the Year

354. I have an host of enemies
          C. M. D.   4 sts.   [Thomas Shepherd]
          1693 Penetential Cries, No. XV, p. 25
          No tune given but intended to be sung

355. I have wandred like a sheep that's lost
          66 octosyllables   Thomas Heywood
          1635 The Hierarchie of the Blessed Angells, pp.
          108-109

356. I pant towards thee
          See: My soul doth pant   Jeremy Taylor
          tow'rds thee

357.   I praise Him most, I love Him best, all praise and
           love is his
              See: Let folly praise that   Robert Southwell
              fancy loves

358.   I read the sins are clouds
              S. M. D.   5 sts.   [John Mason]
              S. M.   1 st.
              1693 Penetential Cries, No. V, p. 9
              Suggested tune: Psalm 25

359.   I sojourn in a vale of tears
              C. M. D.   9 sts.   John Mason
              1683 Spiritual Songs, No. XXX, pp. 63-66
                 st. 2, ℓ. 5: "And dost thou come, my dearest
                 Lord"
                 st. 3, ℓ. 1: "Come then my dearest, dearest
                 Lord"
                 st. 4, ℓ. 1: "What have I in this barren land"
                 st. 4, ℓ. 5: "My Jesus is gone up to heaven"
              No tune given but intended to be sung

360.   I sought thee round about, O thou my God
              10.4.10.4.10.4.10.10 (14 sts.)Thomas Heywood
              1635 The Hierarchie of the Blessed Angells,
                 pp. 53-56
              1931 Songs of Praise, with tune,
                 No. 534   Gustav Holst
                 st. 14, ℓ. 1: "O make us apt to seek, and
                 quick to find"
              *1840 Martineau's Hymns

361.   I thank thee Lord, I thee adore
              L. M. D.   3 sts.   George Wither
              1641 Hal. Pt. 1, No. XXVIII, pp. 46-47
              Suggested tune: Psalm 100

362.   I that am drawn out of the depth
              C. M. D.   5 sts.   John Mason
              C. M.   1 st.
              1683 Spiritual Songs, No. XXVIII, pp. 59-61
                 st. 4, ℓ. 1: "God's furnace doth in Sion stand"
              No tune given but intended to be sung

363.   I wake, and join with you blest spirits above
              irreg.   7 sts.   Lancelot Addison
              1699 Devotional Poems, pp. 42-43

364.   *I wake, I wake, ye heavenly choirs
    See: Awake my soul, and with Thomas Ken
     the sun

365.   I well perceive, that God hath limb'd
    C. M. D.   9 sts.   George Wither
   1641 Hal. Pt. 1, No. CI, pp. 198-200
   Suggested tune: Magnificat

366.   I, whom of late
    4. 6. 4. 6. 4. 6. 4. 6. 8 sts. George Wither
   1641 Hal. Pt. 3, No. LVII, pp. 471-473
   No tune given but intended to be sung

367.   **I would not die but live, dear Living Lord!
    **14 decasyllables   Barnaby Barnes
  **1595 A Divine Centurie of Spirituall Sonnets
   1815 Reprint, p. 26

368.   *I would not wake nor rise again
    See: Awake my soul, and with Thomas Ken
     the sun

369.   If angels sung a Saviour's birth
    C. M.   8 sts.
   1715 Divine Companion, 3rd ed., Jer. Clarke
     p. 20

370.   If by the signs foresee we may
    8. 8. 8. 8. 8. 8 12 sts. George Wither
   1641 Hal. Pt. 1, No. LIX, pp. 108-111
   Suggested tune: Pater Noster

371.   If ever me thou love
    6. 6. 6. 6   32 ℓℓ. Timothy Kendall
   1577 Trifles, pp. 11-12

372.   If I demand what mercy is
    C. M.   9 sts.   William Hunnis
   1597 A Poore Widowes Mite, bound with Seven
     Sobs of a Sorrowful Soule for Sinne, pp. 36-
     38
   Tune in same volume   William Hunnis

373.   If I into myself turn not mine eyes
    10. 10. 10. 10 19 sts. Thomas Heywood
   1635 The Hierarchie of the Blessed Angells,
     pp. 327-329

374.   If it be so that we must fight
             8. 8. 8. 8. 8. 8   John Quarles
         1663 Divine Meditations... With... Divine Ejacula-
             tions, p. 176

375.   If joy be made, when men are born
             C. M. D.   4 sts.   George Wither
         1641 Hal. Pt. 1, No. LXXXVI, pp. 162-163
         Suggested tune: Psalm 23

376.   If men think meanly, O my soul, of thee
             See: Celestial virtue! Yet   Lancelot Addison
             there are but few

377.   If that a sinners sighs be angels' food
             10. 10. 10. 8. 10. 10
         1588 Psalmes, Sonets, and Songs of Sadness,
             No. XXX
         Tune in same volume   William Byrd

378.   **If that sweet spirit of omnipotence
             **14 decasyllables   Barnaby Barnes
         **1595 A Divine Centurie of Spirituall Sonnets
         1815 Reprint, p. 46

379.   If this world's friends might see but once
             L. M.   12 sts.   Henry Vaughan
         1655 Silex Scintillans, Pt. II, pp. 40-42
             st. 11, ℓ. 1: "What needs a conscience calm
             and bright"

380.   If those physicians honour'd be
             L. M. D.   3 sts.   George Wither
         1623 Hymns and Songs, No. LXXVII
         Tune in same volume: Song 44   Orlando Gibbons

381.   Immortal heart, O let thy greater flame
             10. 10. 10. 10   3 sts.   George Herbert
             2 decasyllables
         1633 The Temple, p. 46

382.   Immortal praise be given
             S. M.   8 sts.   Joseph Stennett
         1697 Hys. in Commem., No. XI, p. 13
         Suggested tune: Psalm 25
         From this: "We'll praise our risen Lord"

383.   In all extremes, Lord, thou are still
               8. 8. 8. 8. 8. 8   John Quarles
            1663 Divine Meditations... With... Divine Ejacula-
                  tions, p. 131

384.   In grateful hymns, ye saints display
               L. M.   8 sts.   Joseph Stennett
            1697 Hys. in Commem., No. X, p. 11
            Suggested tune: Psalm 100

385.   *In Paschal feast, ye end of ancient rite
              *Add MS. 10422 at f. 17b.,   Robert Southwell
             British Museum

386.   **In pow'r or wisdom to contend with thee
              **10. 10. 8. 10. 10. 10 (3 sts.) Seventeenth Century
            1754 C. H. C. G., Pt. I, No. 488, p. 286
            Tune to be selected by meter from appended
            Table of Metres and Tunes

387.   In that a master, I was made
               L. M. D.   5 sts.   George Wither
            1641 Hal. Pt. 3, No. VII, pp. 364-366
            Suggested tune: Psalm 100

388.   In the hour of my distress
               7. 7. 7. 6   12 sts.   Robert Herrick
            1647 Noble Numbers, pp. 11-12
          *1819 Selection of Psalms and Hymns, with tune,
                 Cotterill
            1897 Westminster Abbey, with tune,
                 No. 394   M. B. Foster

389.   In the time of my distress
               See: In the hour of my dis-   Robert Herrick
                  tress

390.   In thee I (we) live and move and am (are)
               See: Thou Lord, who raised'st   John Mason
                  heaven and earth

391.   In this world (the Isle of Dreames)
               7. 7. 7. 3   6 sts.   Robert Herrick
            1647 Noble Numbers, pp. 46-47
            1931 Songs of Praise, with tune,
                 No. 348   Gustav Holst

392.   In times of want, we feel what bliss
             C. M. D.   5 sts.   George Wither
         1641 Hal. Pt. 1, No. LV, pp. 97-98
             Suggested tune: Psalm 22

393.   In way of nourishment and strength
             See: Not in rich furniture,   George Herbert
             or fine array

394.   *In vain, Great God, in vain I try
             *1687 A Collection of Miscellanies   John Norris
             *1873 Hymns of Praise and Prayer, ed. James
             Martineau

395.   Inform'd we are, Oh Lord!
             S. M. D.   12 sts.   George Wither
         1641 Hal. Pt. 2, No. LX, pp. 339-342
             Suggested tune: Psalm 25

396.   **Innocent Lamb! thou knew'st thy en'mies plot
             **10.4.4.8.8.10.10.4.4.4.10 (7 sts.) [Faithfull Teate]
         1754 C. H. C. G., Pt. I, No. 389, pp. 226-227
             Tune to be selected by meter from appended
             Table of Metres and Tunes

397.   Is not the hand of God in this
             C. M. D.   4 sts.   John Mason
         1683 Spiritual Songs, No. IX, pp. 21-23
             No tune given but intended to be sung

398.   It is Lord, of thy grace
             S. M. D.   7 sts.   George Wither
         1641 Hal. Pt. 3, No. L, pp. 454-456
             Suggested tune: Psalm 25

399.   It is the common guise of such
             C. M. D.   8 sts.   George Wither
         1641 Hal. Pt. 3, No. X, pp. 368-370
             Suggested tune: Psalm 23

400.   It is too much, that, in my heart
             C. M. D.   6 sts.   George Wither
         1641 Hal. Pt. 3, No. LIII, pp. 465-467
             Suggested tune: Psalm 15

401.   It must be drunk, the cup is mix'd!
             See: The lamb is eaten, and   Jeremy Taylor
             is yet again

402.   It was thy pleasure, Lord, to say
         L. M. D.   7 sts.   George Wither
         1623 Hymnes and Songs, No. LXXX, p. 55
         Tune in same volume: Song 44   Orlando Gibbons

403.   **It will go hard with you saith Christ
         **C. M.   16 sts.   [Robert Smith]
         1754 C. H. C. G., Pt. I, No. 350, pp. 211-212
         Tune to be selected by meter from appended
         Table of Metres and Tunes

404.   I've found the pearl of greatest price
         C. M. D.   4 sts.   John Mason
         C. M.   1 st.
         1683 Spiritual Songs, No. XIII, pp. 28-30
         No tune given but intended to be sung
         1810 A New Selection of 700 Hymns, p. 116
         Any C. M. tune

405.   Jehovah, we in hymns of praise
         C. M.   5 sts.   Joseph Stennett
         1697 Hys. in Commem., No. I, p. 1
         No tune given but intended to be sung

406.   *Jerusalem on high
         See: Sweet place, sweet   Samuel Crossman
               place alone

407.   Jesu, no more, it is full tide
         L. M.   10 sts.   Richard Crashaw
         1646 Steps to the Temple, pp. 23-24
         st. 3, ℓ. 1: "Thy restless feet now cannot go"
         1754 C. H. C. G., Pt. I, No. 399, p. 230
         L. M.   5 sts.
         Tune to be selected by meter from appended
         Table of Metres and Tunes

408.   Jesu, who from thy Father's throne
         8. 8. 6. 8. 8. 6   6 sts.   John Austin
         1672 (1st ed. 1668) Devotions, No. XXIX, pp.
         249-250
         1701 Devot. ed. H., p. 332; tune p. 10, separate
         section

409.   Jesu, whose grace inspires thy priests
         8. 8. 6. 8. 8. 6   6 sts.   John Austin

1672 (1st ed. 1668) <u>Devotions,</u> No. XXXI, pp.
   280-281
1701 <u>Devot.</u> ed. H., p. 375; tune p. 10, separate
   section

410.   Jesus, my life! how shall I truly love thee
        22 decasyllables   Henry Vaughan
        1655 <u>Silex Scintillans,</u> Pt. II, p. 16

411.   **Jesus! O word divinely sweet
        **C. M.   6 sts.   Joseph Stennett
        1709 Hys. in Commem., 3rd ed., No. 47
        1804 <u>Rippon,</u> No. CCCCLXXV
        Suggested tune: <u>Crowley etc.</u>

412.   Job's custom, well deserveth praise
        C. M. D.   5 sts.   George Wither
        1641 <u>Hal.</u> Pt. 3, No. XIII, pp. 375-376
        Suggested tune: <u>Psalm 1</u>

413.   Joy of my life! while left me here
        8.4.8.4.4.4.4.4   4 sts.   Henry Vaughan
        1650 <u>Silex Scintillans,</u> pp. 38-39

414.   Judge not my actions by thy laws
        8.8.8.8.8.8   John Quarles
        1663 <u>Divine Meditations... With... Divine Ejacula-</u>
           <u>tions,</u> p. 172

415.   Just God of vengeance, cast an eye
        8.8.8.8.8.8   John Quarles
        1663 <u>Divine Meditations... With... Divine Ejacula-</u>
           <u>tions,</u> p. 156

416.   Just judge of earth, in whom we trust
        8.8.8.8.8.8   John Quarles
        1663 <u>Divine Meditations... With... Divine Ejacula-</u>
           <u>tions,</u> p. 128

417.   Keep me throughout my life, Oh Lord
        L. M. D.   4 sts.   George Wither
        1641 <u>Hal.</u> Pt. 3, No. XXXI, pp. 414-415
        Suggested tune: <u>10 Com.</u>

418.   Kill me not ev'ry day
        6.10.8.6.10   3 sts.   George Herbert
        1633 <u>The Temple,</u> pp. 53-54

1754 C.H.C.G., Pt. I, No. 373, p. 218
L. M.   3 sts.
Begins: "What helps it, to kill me each day"
Tune to be selected by meter from appended
Table of Metres and Tunes

419.   Kindle O Lord, my love with zeal
         8. 8. 8. 8. 8. 8   John Quarles
         1663 Divine Meditations... With... Divine Ejacula-
              tions, p. 170

420.   King of comforts! King of life
         7. 4. 7. 4   8 sts.   Henry Vaughan
         4. 4. 5. 4. 4. 5   4 sts.
         1650 Silex Scintillans, pp. 76-77

421.   King of glory, King of peace / I will love thee
         7. 4. 7. 4   7 sts.   George Herbert
         1633 The Temple, p. 140
         1737 Collection of Psalms and Hymns, No. XX,
              p. 21
         8. 6. 8. 6   7 sts.
         No tune given but intended to be sung

422.   King of glory, king of peace / With the one, make war
              to cease
         16 septisyllables   George Herbert
         1633 The Temple, p. 192

423.   King of mercy, king of love
         20 septisyllables   Henry Vaughan
         1650 Silex Scintillans, pp. 109-110

424.   Let all the world in every corner sing
         10. 4   Chorus   George Herbert
         6. 6. 6. 6   2 sts.
         1633 The Temple, p. 45
         *1871 S. P. C. K., with tune

425.   Let all who love our Saviour's name
         L. M.   9 sts.   Joseph Stennett
         1697 Hys. in Commem., No. XXXII, p. 41
         Suggested tune: Psalm 100

426.   Let every wonder that I see
         8. 8. 8. 8. 8. 8   John Quarles
         1663 Divine Meditations... With... Divine Ejacula-
              tions, p. 169

427.   **Let folly praise that fancy loves
           **C. M.   8 sts.   Robert Southwell
         **1634 Saint Peter's Complaint etc., pp. 55-56
           1856 Reprint
             st. 2, ℓ. 1: "I praise him most, I love him
             best"

428.   **Let go the whore of Babilon
           **8. 6. 9. 7. 8. 8. 8. 6   11 sts.   Unknown
         **c.1539 Goostly Psalmes and Spirituall Songs
           1846 Remains of Miles Coverdale, with tune,
             pp. 586-588

429.   Let my confession lanch my sore
           8. 8. 8. 8. 8. 8   John Quarles
           1663 Divine Meditations... With... Divine Ejacula-
             tions, p. 137

430.   Let no uncomely censures pass
           8. 8. 8. 8. 8. 8   4 sts.   George Wither
           1641 Hal. Pt. 2, No. LV, pp. 329-330
           Suggested tune: Lords Prayer

431.   Let others boast in gold, and prize
           8. 8. 8. 8. 8. 8   John Quarles
           1663 Divine Meditations... With... Divine Ejacula-
             tions, p. 144

432.   Let others take their course
           S. M.   8 sts.; Amen   John Austin
           1672 (1st ed. 1668) Devotions, No. X, pp. 95-96
             st. 3, ℓ. 1: "Sweet Jesus is the name"
           1671 Psalms and Hymns, with
             tune, pp. 28-29   John Playford

433.   Let shame be their due recompense
           8. 8. 8. 8. 8. 8   John Quarles
           1663 Divine Meditations... With... Divine Ejacula-
             tions, p. 150

434.   Let the most blessed be my guide
           C. M.   12 ℓ ℓ.   John Bunyan
           1744 (1st ed. 1684) Pilgrims Progress, Pt. II,
             p. 18

435.   Let them go court what joys they please
           C. M.   7 sts.; Amen   John Austin

1672 (1st ed. 1668) <u>Devotions,</u> No. XV, pp. 136-
137
1701 <u>Devot.</u> ed. H., with tune, p. 177

436.   Life is a shade, my days
        See: My life's a shade,   Samuel Crossman
        my days

437.   **Life of my soul, bright Lord of love
        **8.8.8   21 sts.   Joseph Beaumont
    **c.1643 <u>Minor Poems,</u> MS.
    1914 <u>Reprint,</u> pp. 1-3

438.   **Lift up to heav'n, sad wretch, thy heavy spirit
        **10.10.10.10.10.10   2 sts. Thomas Campion
    **1613 <u>Two Bookes of Ayres,</u> Bk. I, No. XII
        **Tune in same volume   Thomas Campion
    1909 <u>Campion's Works,</u> pp. 122-123

439.   **Lift up your heads great gates, and sing
        **12 octosyllables and   Joseph Beaumont
        Hallelujahs
    **c.1643 <u>Minor Poems,</u> MS.
        **Marked: To a Base and 2 Trebles
    1914 Reprint, p. 189
    1947 <u>Hymn Book of the King's School,</u> No. 135
    No tune given but intended to be sung

440.   Light thou the lamps, great God, that they
        8.8.8.8.8.8   John Quarles
    1663 <u>Divine Meditations...With...Divine Ejacula-
tions,</u> p. 169

441.   Like as the guilty prisoner stands
        C.M.   9 sts.   William Hunnis
    1597 <u>A Poore Widowes Mite,</u> bound with <u>Seven
Sobs of a Sorrowfull Soule for Sinne,</u> pp. 39-
40
    Tune in same volume   William Hunnis

442.   **Like as the thief in prison cast
        **8.6.8.6.6.6.8.6 6 sts. Humphrey Gifford
    1845 <u>Farr,</u> Vol. 1, p. 217

443.   *Like to the damask rose
        *1634-35 <u>Emblems,</u> Vol. III,   Francis Quarles
        p. <u>285</u>

444.   Listen sweet dove unto my song
            8. 8. 8. 10. 10   7 sts.   George Herbert
         1633 The Temple, pp. 51-52
         1754 C. H. C. G., Pt. I, No. 361, p. 214
         L. M.   3 sts.
         Tune to be selected by meter from appended
         Table of Metres and Tunes

445.   Lo! man rebels, and for one taste doth choose
            See: Almighty God, when   Sir Matthew Hale
            he had rais'd the frame

446.   Lo, now my love appears, my tears
            10. 10. 10. 10   7 sts.   [Christopher Harvey]
         1640 The Synagogue, pp. 22-24

447.   **Lo! Peter weeps, that he his Lord deny'd
            **10. 10   8 sts.   Seventeenth Century
         1754 C. H. C. G., Pt. I, No. 491, p. 288
         Tune to be selected by meter from appended
         Table of Metres and Tunes

448.   Lodg'd in an inn
            See: The blessed Virgin   [Jeremy Taylor]
            travail'd without pain

449.   **Long have I viewed, long have I thought
            **8. 8. 8. 8. 8. 8   6 sts.   *John Norris
         *1687 A Collection of Miscellanies
          1754 C. H. C. G., Pt. I, No. 529, p. 301
          Tune to be selected by meter from appended
          Table of Metres and Tunes

450.   Look down, blest Virgin! and bid justice stay
            10. 10. 10. 10   2 sts.   Benjamin Keach
         1681 Sion in Distress, 2nd ed., p. 90

451.   Look forth mine eye; look up and view
            L. M. D.   5 sts.   George Wither
         1641 Hal. Pt. 1, No. III, pp. 5-6
            Suggested tunes: Lamentation or Psalm 51

452.   Look hither, ye whose taste
            See: Come ye hither all,   George Herbert
            whose taste

453.   Lord, cast thine eyes upon thy foes

8. 8. 8. 8. 8. 8   John Quarles
1663 Divine Meditations... With... Divine Ejaculations, p. 153

454.   Lord, cleanse my heart, and guide my tongue
       8. 8. 8. 8. 8. 8   John Quarles
       1663 Divine Meditations... With... Divine Ejacula-
       tions, p. 132

455.   Lord, come away; why dost thou stay
       irreg.   20 ℓℓ.; Amen Jeremy Taylor
       1655 Festival Hymnes appended to The Golden
            Grove, p. 147
       *1827 Hymns Written and adapted to the Weekly
            Church Service, Posth. ed. of Raymond
            Heber
       1852 Hys. for the Christian Ch. and Hm.,
            No. 212
       Rewritten form: "Descend to thy Jerusalem,
       O Lord" or "Draw nigh to thy Jerusalem,
       O Lord"
       Choice of tunes from other books

456.   Lord, crush my lion-hearted foes
       8. 8. 8. 8. 8. 8   John Quarles
       1663 Divine Meditations... With... Divine Ejacula-
       tions, p. 130

457.   Lord, curb my tongue, and make me see
       8. 8. 8. 8. 8. 8   John Quarles
       1663 Divine Meditations... With... Divine Ejacula-
       tions, p. 140

458.   Lord, every creature writes a story
       8. 8. 8. 8. 8. 8   John Quarles
       1663 Divine Meditations... With... Divine Ejacula-
       tions, p. 160

459.   Lord, for the mercies of the night
       See: My God was with me all   John Mason
       this night

460.   Lord, from the noisome sink of sin
       C. M. D.   4 sts.   George Wither
       1641 Hal. Pt. 3, No. XXXIIII, pp. 419-421
       Suggested tune: We praise thee God

461.   Lord, give me a believing heart
          8. 8. 8. 8. 8. 8   John Quarles
          1663 Divine Meditations... With... Divine Ejacula-
               tions, p. 166

462.   Lord God, from whom all mercy springs
          8. 8. 8. 8. 8. 8   John Quarles
          1663 Divine Meditations... With... Divine Ejacula-
               tions, p. 147

463.   Lord God of gods, before whose throne
          8. 8. 8. 8. 8. 8   John Quarles
          1663 Divine Meditations... With... Divine Ejacula-
               tions, p. 143

464.   **Lord God with all my heart, and soul, and mind
          **10. 10   6 sts.   Seventeenth Century
          1754 C. H. C. G., Pt. I, No. 518, p. 298
          Tune to be selected by meter from appended
          Table of Metres and Tunes

465.   Lord, guide my footsteps in thy truth
          8. 8. 8. 8. 8. 8   John Quarles
          1663 Divine Meditations... With... Divine Ejacula-
               tions, p. 135

466.   Lord, had not man sought out by sin
          C. M. D.   5 sts.   George Wither
          1641 Hal. Pt. 1, No. III, pp. 6-8
          Suggested tunes: Mag. or Te Deum

467.   Lord, hear my troubled voice, and bring
          8. 8. 8. 8. 8. 8   John Quarles
          1663 Divine Meditations... With... Divine Ejacula-
               tions, p. 147

468.   Lord, help me when my griefs do call
          8. 8. 8. 8. 8. 8   John Quarles
          1663 Divine Meditations... With... Divine Ejacula-
               tions, p. 142

469.   Lord, hide me from my bloody foes
          8. 8. 8. 8. 8. 8   John Quarles
          1663 Divine Meditations... With... Divine Ejacula-
               tions, p. 148

470.   Lord, how divine's this gift of thine

C. M.   6 sts.   Joseph Stennett
1697 Hys. in Commem., No. XIII, p. 15
No tune given but intended to be sung

471.   Lord, how dreadfull is this hour
        7.7.7.7.7.7.7.7.7.7.7   6 sts. George Wither
        1641 Hal. Pt. 1, No. XXVI, pp. 41-43
        No tune given but intended to be sung

472.   Lord, how I long to see thy face
        8.8.8.8.8.8   John Quarles
        1663 Divine Meditations...With...Divine Ejacula-
             tions, p. 147

473.   Lord, how in silence I despise
        See: Lord, in my silence   George Herbert
        how do I despise

474.   *Lord, I have cast up the account
        *1681 Poetical Fragments, pp. 51-61 John Mason
        *From this: "He wants not friends"

475.   Lord, I have sinn'd! and such the sum
        See: Lord, I have sinn'd   Jeremy Taylor
        and the black number swells

476.   Lord, I have sinn'd, and the black number swells
        irreg.   17 ℓℓ.; Amen   Jeremy Taylor
        1655 Penententiall Hymns, appended to The Golden
             Grove, pp. 166-167
        1688 Harmonia Sacra, with
             tune, pp. 50-51   Pelham Humphryes

477.   Lord, I love, and I adore
        7.8.7.8.7.8.7.8.8.8.8.8   Lancelot Addison
        1699 Devotional Poems, p. 50

478.   Lord if mine eyes should look too high
        8.8.8.8.8.8   John Quarles
        1663 Divine Meditations...With...Divine Ejacula-
             tions, p. 168

479.   Lord, if my tongue and busy quill
        8.8.8.8.8.8   John Quarles
        1663 Divine Meditations...With...Divine Ejacula-
             tions, p. 170

480.   Lord, if our enemies increase
         8. 8. 8. 8. 8. 8   John Quarles
         1663 Divine Meditations... With... Divine Ejacula-
         tions, p. 129

481.   Lord, if the signs may trusted be
         L. M. D.   4 sts.   George Wither
         1641 Hal. Pt. 1, No. XLVI, pp. 76-77
         Suggested tune: 10 Com.

482.   Lord, if thou take away thy hand
         8. 8. 8. 8. 8. 8   John Quarles
         1663 Divine Meditations... With... Divine Ejacula-
         tions, p. 144

483.   Lord, if thy flame must needs be felt
         8. 8. 8. 8. 8. 8   John Quarles
         1663 Divine Meditations... With... Divine Ejacula-
         tions, p. 148

484.   Lord, if thy mercies purge my heart
         8. 8. 8. 8. 8. 8   John Quarles
         1663 Divine Meditations... With... Divine Ejacula-
         tions, p. 143

485.   Lord, if thy pleasure make me poor
         8. 8. 8. 8. 8. 8   John Quarles
         1663 Divine Meditations... With... Divine Ejacula-
         tions, p. 140

486.   Lord, in my silence how do I despise
         10. 4. 10. 4. 7. 6. 10. 4   3 sts.   George Herbert
         1633 The Temple, pp. 62-63
         1737 Collection of Psalms and Hymns, No. XII,
         p. 49
         8. 6. 8. 6   9 sts.
         Begins: "Lord, how in silence I despise"
         No tune given but intended to be sung

487.   Lord, in the day thou art about
         See: My God, my only help and   John Mason
         hope

488.   Lord, in thy name, and in thy fear
         C. M. D.   6 sts.   George Wither
         1641 Hal. Pt. 1, No. XLIIII, pp. 72-74
         Suggested tune: Te Deum

489. Lord, in thy wrath correct me not
        8. 8. 8. 8. 8. 8   John Quarles
        1663 Divine Meditations... With... Divine Ejacula-
            tions, p. 139

490. Lord, it belongs not to my care
        See: My whole, though broken   Richard Baxter
        heart, O Lord

491. *Lord, it is not for us to care
        See: My whole, though broken   Richard Baxter
        heart, O Lord

492. Lord! it hath pleased thee to say
        L. M. D.   7 sts.   George Wither
        1641 Hal. Pt. 2, No. XXIIII, pp. 274-276
        Suggested tunes: 10 Com. or Lamentation

493. Lord Jesus! with what sweetness and delight
        irreg.   62 ℓ ℓ.   Henry Vaughan
        1655 Silex Scintillans, Part II, pp. 1-3

494. Lord keep me from my self that am
        8. 8. 8. 8. 8. 8   John Quarles
        1663 Divine Meditations... With... Divine Ejacula-
            tions, p. 171

495. Lord, keep me from those hearts and tongues
        8. 8. 8. 8. 8. 8   John Quarles
        1663 Divine Meditations... With... Divine Ejacula-
            tions, p. 146

496. Lord, keep me just and judge my right
        8. 8. 8. 8. 8. 8   John Quarles
        1663 Divine Meditations... With... Divine Ejacula-
            tions, p. 135

497. Lord, leave us not too long a space
        8. 8. 8. 8. 8. 8   John Quarles
        1663 Divine Meditations... With... Divine Ejacula-
            tions, p. 130

498. Lord let mine eyes not sleep until
        8. 8. 8. 8. 8. 8   John Quarles
        1663 Divine Meditations... With... Divine Ejacula-
            tions, p. 168

499.   Lord, let our Jesus, and thy Christ
             8. 8. 8. 8. 8. 8   John Quarles
             1663 Divine Meditations... With... Divine Ejacula-
                 tions, p. 157

500.   Lord, let the evening of my grief
             8. 8. 8. 8. 8. 8   John Quarles
             1663 Divine Meditations... With... Divine Ejacula-
                 tions, p. 137

501.   Lord let the fire of my true zeal
             8. 8. 8. 8. 8. 8   John Quarles
             1663 Divine Meditations... With... Divine Ejacula-
                 tions, p. 165

502.   Lord let the flames of holy charity
             See: Tongues of fire from   Jeremy Taylor
             heaven descend

503.   Lord let the morning of my grief
             8. 8. 8. 8. 8. 8   John Quarles
             1663 Divine Meditations... With... Divine Ejacula-
                 tions, p. 175

504.   Lord let the praises of thy power
             8. 8. 8. 8. 8. 8   John Quarles
             1663 Divine Meditations... With... Divine Ejacula-
                 tions, p. 176

505.   Lord, let the sunshine of thy face
             8. 8. 8. 8. 8. 8   John Quarles
             1663 Divine Meditations... With... Divine Ejacula-
                 tions, p. 138

506.   Lord, let the words we hear this day
             C. M. D.   3 sts.   George Wither
             1641 Hal. Pt. 1, No. XXXVII, pp. 59-60
             Suggested tune: Psalm 4 or 117

507.   Lord, let thy favor still inflame
             8. 8. 8. 8. 8. 8   John Quarles
             1663 Divine Meditations... With... Divine Ejacula-
                 tions, p. 149

508.   Lord, let thy fury cease to burn
             8. 8. 8. 8. 8. 8   John Quarles
             1663 Divine Meditations... With... Divine Ejacula-
                 tions, p. 154

509.   Lord, let thy judgments fill all those
               8. 8. 8. 8. 8. 8   John Quarles
            1663 Divine Meditations... With... Divine Ejacula-
                  tions, p. 142

510.   Lord, let thy name secure and free
               8. 8. 8. 8. 8. 8   John Quarles
            1663 Divine Meditations... With... Divine Ejacula-
                  tions, p. 144

511.   Lord, let thy pow'r protect the king
               10 octosyllables 3 sts.   George Wither
            1641 Hal. Pt. 1, No. LXXXIIII, pp. 159-160
            No tune given but intended to be sung

512.   Lord, let thy sacred fire thaw
               8. 8. 8. 8. 8. 8   John Quarles
            1663 Divine Meditations... With... Divine Ejacula-
                  tions, p. 175

513.   Lord let thy wonders, and thy ways
               8. 8. 8. 8. 8. 8   John Quarles
            1663 Divine Meditations... With... Divine Ejacula-
                  tions, p. 161

514.   Lord, living, here we are
               S. M. D.   5 sts.   George Wither
            1641 Hal. Pt. 2, No. XVII, pp. 261-262
            Suggested tune: Psalm 25

515.   Lord, make the torments we endure
               8. 8. 8. 8. 8. 8   John Quarles
            1663 Divine Meditations... With... Divine Ejacula-
                  tions, p. 127

516.   Lord, many times thou pleased art
               C. M. D.   11 sts.   George Wither
            1641 Hal. Pt. 3, No. LXI, pp. 481-484
            Suggested tune: We praise thee God

517.   *Lord, may we feel no anxious care
               See: My whole, though   Richard Baxter
               broken heart, O Lord

518.   *Lord, now my sleep does me forsake
               See: My God, now I from sleep   Thomas Ken
               awake

519.   Lord now the time returns
            S. M.   8 sts.; Amen   John Austin
        1672 (1st ed. 1668) Devotions, No. XXXII,
            pp. 287-288
        1701 Devot. ed. H., p. 385; tune p. 9, separate
            section
            **Abridged form begins: "Blessed be thy love"

520.   Lord of my life, length of my days
            C. M. D.   4 sts.   John Mason
        1683 Spiritual Songs, No. XXIX, pp. 61-63
        No tune given but intended to be sung

521.   Lord! on this day, thou dids't bestow
            C. M. D.   7 sts.   George Wither
        1641 Hal. Pt. 2, No. XII, pp. 250-252
        Suggested tune: Magnificat

522.   Lord, our fathers found redress
            8. 8. 8. 8. 8. 8   John Quarles
        1663 Divine Meditations... With... Divine Ejacula-
            tions, p. 141

523.   Lord, plant thy fear before my eyes
            8. 8. 8. 8. 8. 8   John Quarles
        1663 Divine Meditations... With... Divine Ejacula-
            tions, p. 162

524.   Lord plant my fears within my breast
            8. 8. 8. 8. 8. 8   John Quarles
        1663 Divine Meditations... With... Divine Ejacula-
            tions, p. 167

525.   Lord, plead my cause, and right my wrong
            8. 8. 8. 8. 8. 8   John Quarles
        1663 Divine Meditations... With... Divine Ejacula-
            tions, p. 138

526.   Lord, purge my heart, and cleanse my hand
            8. 8. 8. 8. 8. 8   John Quarles
        1663 Divine Meditations... With... Divine Ejacula-
            tions, p. 135

527.   Lord, purge my soul, that I may learn
            8. 8. 8. 8. 8. 8   John Quarles
        1663 Divine Meditations... With... Divine Ejacula-
            tions, p. 156

528.   Lord, right my wrongs, and plead my right
              8. 8. 8. 8. 8. 8   John Quarles
              1663 Divine Meditations... With... Divine Ejacula-
              tions, p. 141

529.   Lord, rise in power within my heart
              8. 8. 8. 8. 8. 8   John Quarles
              1663 Divine Meditations... With... Divine Ejacula-
              tions, p. 149

530.   Lord, save me from my foes; make void
              8. 8. 8. 8. 8. 8   John Quarles
              1663 Divine Meditations... With... Divine Ejacula-
              tions, p. 146

531.   Lord, season my unsavory spirit
              8. 8. 8. 8. 8. 8   John Quarles
              1663 Divine Meditations... With... Divine Ejacula-
              tions, p. 174

532.   Lord, should the sun, the clouds, the wind
              C. M. D.   4 sts.   George Wither
              1623 Hymns and Songs, No. LXXXV, p. 59
              Tune in same volume: Song 3   Orlando Gibbons

533.   Lord, should we oft forget to sing
              L. M. D.   5 sts.   George Wither
              1641 Hal. Pt. 1, No. XVII, pp. 24-26
              Suggested tune: Prayer after the Command-
              ments

534.   Lord, shoulds't thou punish every sin
              8. 8. 8. 8. 8. 8   John Quarles
              1663 Divine Meditations... With... Divine Ejacula-
              tions, p. 160

535.   Lord, since there must be always foes
              8. 8. 8. 8. 8. 8   John Quarles
              1663 Divine Meditations... With... Divine Ejacula-
              tions, p. 167

536.   Lord, teach me to renown thy name
              8. 8. 8. 8. 8. 8   John Quarles
              1663 Divine Meditations... With... Divine Ejacula-
              tions, p. 131

537.   Lord, teach me wisely to contemn

8. 8. 8. 8. 8. 8   John Quarles
1663 Divine Meditations... With... Divine Ejaculations, p. 143

538.   Lord, teach my heart to walk upright
         8. 8. 8. 8. 8. 8   John Quarles
         1663 Divine Meditations... With... Divine Ejacula-
         tions, p. 159

539.   Lord, teach my humble eyes the art
         8. 8. 8. 8. 8. 8   John Quarles
         1663 Divine Meditations... With... Divine Ejacula-
         tions, p. 162

540.   Lord, teach my reins, that in the night
         8. 8. 8. 8. 8. 8   John Quarles
         1663 Divine Meditations... With... Divine Ejacula-
         tions, p. 132

541.   Lord, teach our loyal hearts to build
         8. 8. 8. 8. 8. 8   John Quarles
         1663 Divine Meditations... With... Divine Ejacula-
         tions, p. 163

542.   Lord, teach us timely how to pray
         8. 8. 8. 8. 8. 8   John Quarles
         1663 Divine Meditations... With... Divine Ejacula-
         tions, p. 128

543.   Lord! that, there might no vacant-place
         C. M. D.   4 sts.   George Wither
         1641 Hal. Pt. 2, No. VI, pp. 235-236
         Suggested tune: Psalm 22

544.   Lord, thou hast fil'd our hearts with joy
         C. M. D.   4 sts.   George Wither
         1641 Hal. Pt. 2, No. XI, pp. 248-249
         Suggested tune: Magnificat

545.   Lord, thou hast given me a cell
         8. 4   58 ℓ ℓ .   Robert Herrick
         1647 Noble Numbers, pp. 13-15

546.   Lord, thou hast giv'n to us
         S. M.   8 sts.   Joseph Stennett
         1697 Hys. in Commem., No. XXXI, p. 40
         Suggested tune: Psalm 25

547.   Lord, thou hast overcome
         S. M. D.   4 sts.   [John Mason]
         1693 Penetential Cries, No. II, p. 5
         Suggested tune: Psalm 25

548.   Lord, thou hast planted me a vine
         C. M. D.   4 sts.   [Thomas Shepherd]
         C. M.   1 st.
         1693 Penetential Cries, No. XXVII, p. 41
         No tune given but intended to be sung

549.   Lord, thou hast told us that there be
         8. 8. 6. 4   9 sts.   Thomas Washbourne
         1654 Divine Poems, pp. 31-32
         1931 Songs of Praise, with tune,
         No. 107   Arnold Bax

550.   Lord, thou that hoard'st thy grace for those
         8. 8. 8. 8. 8. 8   John Quarles
         1663 Divine Meditations... With... Divine Ejacula-
              tions, p. 137

551.   Lord, thou that mad'st me, and do'st pry
         8. 8. 8. 8. 8. 8   John Quarles
         1663 Divine Meditations... With... Divine Ejacula-
              tions, p. 171

552.   Lord, thou that underneath thy wing
         8. 8. 8. 8. 8. 8   John Quarles
         1663 Divine Meditations... With... Divine Ejacula-
              tions, p. 150

553.   Lord, thou whose equal hand allays
         8. 8. 8. 8. 8. 8   John Quarles
         1663 Divine Meditations... With... Divine Ejacula-
              tions, p. 129

554.   Lord, thou whose mercies do exceed
         8. 8. 8. 8. 8. 8   John Quarles
         1663 Divine Meditations... With... Divine Ejacula-
              tions, p. 140

555.   Lord, thou whose mercies fail not those
         8. 8. 8. 8. 8. 8   John Quarles
         1663 Divine Meditations... With... Divine Ejacula-
              tions, p. 155

556.   Lord, thou wilt love me. Wilt thou not
              8. 4. 6. D.   3 sts.   [Christopher Harvey]
              1640 The Synagogue, p. 10

557.   Lord, though I murmur not, at thee
              C. M. D.   6 sts.   George Wither
              1641 Hal. Pt. 1, No. CII, pp. 201-203
              Suggested tune: Magnificat

558.   Lord, though we feel the bitter taste
              8. 8. 8. 8. 8. 8   John Quarles
              1663 Divine Meditations... With... Divine Ejacula-
                   tions, p. 146

559.   Lord, we again lift up our eyes
              C. M.   8 sts.; Amen   John Austin
              1672 (1st ed. 1668) Devotions, No. XXV,
                   pp. 215-216
              1671 Psalms and Hymns, with
                   tune, pp. 82-83   John Playford

560.   Lord, we approach thy throne
              S. M.   8 sts.   Joseph Stennett
              1697 Hys. in Commem., No. XXVII, p. 34
              Suggested tune: Psalm 25

561.   Lord, we are captives, and we bow
              8. 8. 8. 8. 8. 8   John Quarles
              1663 Divine Meditations... With... Divine Ejacula-
                   tions, p. 166

562.   Lord we are several members join'd
              8. 8. 8. 8. 8. 8   John Quarles
              1663 Divine Meditations... With... Divine Ejacula-
                   tions, p. 169

563.   Lord, what a pleasant life were this
              C. M.   9 sts.; Amen   John Austin
              1672 (1st ed. 1668) Devotions, No. XXVII,
                   pp. 240-241
              1701 Devot. ed. H., p. 319; tune p. 1, separate
                   section

564.   Lord, what is man that lump of sin
              C. M. D.   4 sts.   John Mason
              C. M.   1 st.
              1683 Spiritual Songs, No. XVII, pp. 38-39
              No tune given but intended to be sung

565.   Lord, what is man?   Why should he cost you
             irreg.   66 ℓ ℓ .   Richard Crashaw
         1648 Steps to the Temple, pp. 107-109
         1754 C.H.C.G., Pt. I, No. 401, p. 231
         L.M.   6 sts.
         Tune to be selected by meter from appended
         Table of Metres and Tunes

566.   Lord, when a nation thee offends
             8.8.8.8.8.8   George Wither
         1641 Hal. Pt. 1, No. LXXII, pp. 133-134
         Suggested tune: Pater.Noster

567.   Lord when my grief shall find a tongue
             8.8.8.8.8.8   John Quarles
         1663 Divine Meditations...With...Divine Ejacula-
             tions, p. 171

568.   Lord! when those glorious lights I see
             L.M.D.   4 sts.   George Wither
         1641 Hal. Pt. 1, No. XV, pp. 21-22
         Suggested tune: The Lamentation

569.   Lord! when thou didst thy self undress
             8.8.8.8   5 sts.   Henry Vaughan
         1650 Silex Scintillans, p. 29
             st. 4, ℓ . 1: "Ah, my dear Lord! what couldst
             thou spy"

570.   Lord, when we call to mind these things
             C.M.D.   10 sts.   George Wither
         1641 Hal. Pt. 2, No. XIIII, pp. 255-257
         Suggested tune: Psalm 4

571.   **Lord when the wise men came from far
             **8.8.8.8.8.8   6 sts.   Sidney Godolphin
         **Bodleian Library MS. Malone 13, pp. 85-86
         1931 The Poems of Sidney Godolphin (Wm. Digh-
             ton ed.) pp. 28-29

572.   Lord, who hast formed me out of mud
             8.8.8   3 sts.   George Herbert
         1633 The Temple, p. 59
             st. 3, ℓ . 1: "Enrich my heart, mouth, hands
             in me"
         1931 Songs of Praise, with tune,
             No. 401   G.W. Briggs

573.   Lord, who shall dwell above with thee
         C. M.   8 sts.; Amen   John Austin
         1672 (1st ed. 1668) Devotions, No. VII
         1671 Psalms and Hymns, with
              tune, pp. 48-49   John Playford

574.   No entry.

575.   Lord, with what bounty and rare clemency
         10. 8. 6. 8. 6. 10   5 sts.   George Herbert
         1633 The Temple, p. 74
         1754 C. H. C. G., Pt. I, No. 362, pp. 214-215
         9. 9. 7. 7. 9
         Begins: "With what bounty and rare clemency"
         Tune to be selected by meter from appended
         Table of Metres and Tunes

576.   Lord, with what courage and delight
         8. 4. 8. 4. 4. 4. 4. 8.   3 sts.   Henry Vaughan
         1650 Silex Scintillans, pp. 45-46

577.   Lord! with what zeal, did Stephen breath
         L. M. D.   3 sts.   George Wither
         1641 Hal. Pt. 2, No. XLIII, pp. 312-313
         Suggested tune: Pater Noster

578.   Love bade me welcome: Yet my soul drew back
         10. 6. 10. 6. 10. 6   3 sts.   George Herbert
         1633 The Temple, p. 183
         1931 The Hymn Book of the Modern Church,
              p. 111

579.   Love, lift me up upon thy golden wings
         7 decasyllables   41 sts.   Edmund Spenser
         1611 Foure Hymnes "An Hymne of heavenly love"
         st. 25, ℓ . 1: "O blessed well of love! O
              flower of grace"

580.   **Love who each ev'ning makes my bed
         **L. M.   7 sts.   [Faithfull Teate]
         1754 C. H. C. G., Pt. I, No. 392, p. 299
         Tune to be selected by meter from appended
         Table of Metres and Tunes

581.   **Man! watch and pray; the very first
         **C. M.   2 sts.   Seventeenth Century
         1754 C. H. C. G., Pt. I, No. 511, p. 296

Tune to be selected by meter from appended
Table of Metres and Tunes

582.   Man's life a sign, a groan, a cry
          L. M.   6 sts.   Thomas Shepherd
          1743 (16th ed.) Spiritual Songs, No. XXXIV
          No tune given but intended to be sung

583.   Man's lifes a book of history
          See: Now from the altar of our   John Mason
             heart

584.   **May I taste that communion, Lord
          **C. M.   2 sts.   Seventeenth Century
          1754 C. H. C. G., Pt. I, No. 516, p. 298
          Tune to be selected by meter from appended
          Table of Metres and Tunes

585.   Mercy I will and judgement sing
          8. 8. 8. 8. 8. 8   4 sts.   Rt. King
          1701 Divine Companion, with tune,
             p. 33   Robert King

586.   Methinks I feel more perfect rest
          8. 6. 8. 6. 4. 4. 6. 4. 4. 6   4 sts.   George Wither
          1641 Hal. Pt. 1, No. LXXVII, pp. 142-143
          No tune given but intended to be sung

587.   Midnight hymn
          See: My God, I now from   Thomas Ken
             sleep awake

588.   **Mock not, profane despisers of the spirit
          See: Nay, startle not   [Christopher Harvey]
             to hear the rushing wind

589.   Morning Hymn
          See: Awake my soul and with the Thomas Ken
             sun

590.   Most gracious God, do not behold
          C. M.   9 sts.   William Hunnis
          1597 The Poore Widowes Mite, bound with Seven
             Sobs of a Sorrowfull Soule for Sinne,
             pp. 35-36
          Tune in same volume   William Hunnis

591.   Most glorious Lord of life, that on this day
              14 decasyllables   Edmund Spenser
           1611 Amoretti and Epithalamion, Sonnet lxviii
           1906 The English Hymnal with Tunes,
              No. 283   H. Lawes

592.   Most men repute a common inn
              C. M. D.   8 sts.   George Wither
           1641 Hal. Pt. 3, No. LIII, pp. 462-465
           Suggested tune: Psalm 15

593.   Most mighty God, I do confess
              C. M.   9 sts.   William Hunnis
           1597 The Poore Widowes Mite, bound with Seven
              Sobs of a Sorrowfull Soule for Sinne, pp. 38-
              39
           Tune in same volume   William Hunnis

594.   Mournful Judah shrieks and cries
              irreg.   20 ℓℓ.; Amen Jeremy Taylor
           1655 Festival Hymnes appended to the Golden
              Grove, p. 152

595.   **Must Jesus bear the cross alone
              **C. M.   4 sts.   Thomas Shepherd
           1908 The Booke of Common   and David Williams
              Praise, with tune, No. 557   H. Houseley

596.   My blessed Saviour, is thy love
              C. M.   10 sts.   Joseph Stennett
           1697 Hys. in Commem., No. XXII, p. 27
           No tune given but intended to be sung

597.   **My days be few, my sins past number be
              **14 decasyllables   Barnaby Barnes
           **1595 A Divine Centurie of Spirituall Sonnets
           1815 Reprint, p. 21

598.   My dearest Lord and Love! What shall I do
              irreg.   4 sts.   Lancelot Addison
           1699 Devotional Poems, pp. 55-56
           1754 C. H. C. G., Pt. I, No. 513, p. 297
           Tune to be selected by meter from appended
              Table of Metres and Tunes

599.   My God a God of pardon is
              C. M. D.   5 sts.
                                                 John Mason

C. M. D.					5 sts.					John Mason
1683 Spiritual Songs, No. XXII, pp. 48-49
No tune given but intended to be sung

600.	My God and King, to thee
		6. 4. 8. 8. 8. 8			3 sts.					Henry Vaughan
		6. 4
		1655 Silex Scintillans, Pt. II, p. 60

601.	My God, full tears are all the diet
		8. 8. 8. 8. 8. 8						John Quarles
		1663 Divine Meditations... With... Divine Ejacula-
			tions, p. 141

602.	My God, had I my breath from thee
		C. M.					6 sts. ; Amen		John Austin
		1672 (1st ed. 1668) Devotions, No. XIV, pp. 128-
			129
		1671 Psalms and Hymns, with
			tune, pp. 8-9						John Playford

603.	My God, he is the God of grace
		C. M. D.				3 sts.			Thomas Shepherd
		1743 (16th ed.) Spiritual Songs, No. XI
		No tune given but intended to be sung

604.	My God, how gracious art thou! I had slipped
		10. 4					28 ℓℓ .			Henry Vaughan
		1650 Silex Scintillans, p. 51

605.	My God, how kind? how good art thou
		L. M. D.				4 sts.			George Wither
		1641 Hal. Pt. 1, No. XXII, pp. 33-34
		Suggested tune: 10 Com.

606.	My God, I'm wounded by my sin
		8. 8					12 ℓℓ .			Robert Herrick
		8. 8					Chorus
		1647 Noble Numbers, pp. 4-5
		Marked: "An Anthem, sung in the Chappell at
			White-Hall, before the King"

607.	My God, my God, my light, my love
		C. M.					8 sts.			[Thomas Shepherd]
		1693 Penetential Cries, No. XXXII, p. 47
		No tune given but intended to be sung

608.   My God, my only help and hope
            C. M. D.   4 sts.   John Mason
        1683 Spiritual Songs, No. VI, pp. 16-17
            st. 2, ℓ. 1: "Lord, in the day thou art about"

609.   My God, my reconciled God
            C. M. D.   5 sts.   John Mason
        1683 Spiritual Songs, No. XXIII, pp. 50-51
            st. 2, ℓ. 5: "The world can neither give nor
            take"
            st. 5, ℓ. 1: "Where God doth dwell, sure
            Heaven is there"
        No tune given but intended to be sung

610.   *My God, now I from sleep awake
            *L. M.   12 sts.; Doxology   Thomas Ken
        *Sung at Winchester College from 1674
        *1692 Pamphlet with no title page, printed for
            Rich. Smith

611.   My God, to thee ourselves we owe
            L. M.   7 sts.; Amen   John Austin
        1672 (1st ed. 1668) Devotions, No. XXVI, p. 231
        1671 Psalms and Hymns, with tune,
            pp. 72-73   John Playford

612.   My God, thy mercies so abound
            8. 8. 8. 8. 8. 8   John Quarles
        1663 Divine Meditations... With... Divine Ejacula-
            tions, p. 163

613.   My God was with me all this night
            C. M. D.   4 sts.   John Mason
        1683 Spiritual Songs, No. X, pp. 23-24
            st. 4, ℓ. 1: "Lord, for the mercies of the
            night"
        No tune given but intended to be sung

614.   My God, whose fear drives fear away
            8. 8. 8. 8. 8. 8   John Quarles
        1663 Divine Meditations... With... Divine Ejacula-
            tions, p. 136

615.   My grandame Eve, I curse not Lord
            C. M. D.   7 sts.   George Wither
        1641 Hal. Pt. 3, No. XXV, pp. 401-403
        Suggested tune: Psalm 1

616.   My heart lies dead
            See: My stock lies dead   George Herbert

617.   My heart, why art thou sad?
            S. M. D.   9 sts.   George Wither
            1641 Hal. Pt. 1, No. XCII, pp. 177-180
            No tune given but intended to be sung

618.   My hope; and those endeavors, now
            C. M. D.   4 sts.   George Wither
            1641 Hal. Pt. 1, No. CVI, pp. 208-209
            Suggested tune: Psalm 4

619.   My Jesus is gone up to heaven
            See: I sojourn in a vale of   John Mason
                tears

620.   My Jesus, thou that wert no less
            8. 8. 8. 8. 8. 8   John Quarles
            1663 Divine Meditations... With... Divine Ejacula-
            tions, p. 134

621.   My joy, my life, my crown!
            6. 8. 6. 10. 10   4 sts.   George Herbert
            1633 The Temple, pp. 162-163

622.   My life's a shade, my days
            6. 6. 6. 6   6 sts.   Samuel Crossman
            4. 4. 4. 4   Chorus
            1678 The Young Man's Meditations, pp. 421-423
            *1863 Kennedy, Book of Praise, with tune, No.
            CLIII
            Begins: "Life is a shade, my days,"
            1864 The Book of Praise, No. CLIII

623.   My little bird how canst thou sit
            L. M.   14 sts.   John Bunyan
            1686 A Book for Boys and Girls, pp. 40-42
            Tune in same volume   Composer not named

624.   **My Lord at eight days old began to bleed
            **10. 8. 8. 10   [Faithfull Teate]
            1754 C. H. C. G., Pt. I, No. 387, p. 225
            Tune to be selected by meter from appended
            Table of Metres and Tunes

625.   My Lord, my God, I once could sing

      C. M. D.   4 sts.   [Thomas Shepherd]
      C. M.   1 st.
     1693 Penetential Cries, No. XXIII, p. 36
     No tune given but intended to be sung

626.   My Lord, my Life was crucified
       See: My Lord, my Love was   John Mason
       crucified

627.   My Lord my Love was crucified
       C. M. D.   3 sts.   John Mason
       C. M.   1 st.
     1683 Spiritual Songs, No. XIX, pp. 42-43
       Variant ℓ. 1: "My Lord, my Life was Cruci-
       fied"
       st. 2, ℓ. 1: "Thou, Lord, who dayly feed'st
       thy sheep"
     No tune given but intended to be sung

628.   My Lord, (Oh! I can speak no more without a groan)
       irreg.   3 sts.   Lancelot Addison
     1699 Devotional Poems, p. 12

629.   My Lord! what have I brought thee home
       See: Blest be the God of   George Herbert
       love

630.   My love, my life, my dear, my all
       irreg.   4 sts.   Lancelot Addison
     1699 Devotional Poems, pp. 44-45

631.   My Saviour is gone up to heaven
       See: I sojourn in a vale of tears   John Mason

632.   My sins, and follies, Lord, by thee
       C. M. D.   5 sts.   George Wither
     1641 Hal. Pt. 1, No. XCVIII, pp. 192-193
       Suggested tune: Psalm 4

633.   My sins are like the sands upon the shore
       10.10.10.10.10.10   Francis Quarles
     1632 Divine Fancies, Bk. II, No. 69, p. 98

634.   My sins are like the stars, within the skies
       10.10.10.10.10.10   Francis Quarles
     1632 Divine Fancies, Bk. II, No. 72, pp. 99-100

635.   My song is love unknown
            6. 6. 6. 6. 4. 4. 4. 4   7 sts.   Samuel Crossman
        1678 The Young Man's Meditation, pp. 417-419
        *1868 Anglican Hymn Book with tune
        1913 The Institute Hymnal, with
            tune, No. 56   John B. Calkins

636.   My soul doth magnify the Lord
            [This is not the Magnificat]   John Mason
            C. M. D.   5 sts.
            C. M.   1 st.
        1683 Spiritual Songs, No. XXIV, pp. 52-54
            st. 3, ℓ. 1: "There is a stream, which issues
            forth"
        No tune given but intended to be sung

637.   My soul doth pant tow'rds thee
            irreg.   24 ℓℓ.; Amen   Jeremy Taylor
        1655 Festival Hymnes appended to The Golden
            Grove, pp. 155-156
        1754 C. H. C. G., Pt. I, No. 409, p. 233
            5. 6. 5. 6. 2. 6   3 sts.
        Begins: "I pant towards thee"
        Tune to be selected by meter from appended
            Table of Metres and Tunes

638.   My soul go boldly forth
            6. 6. 6. 5. 6. 5   31 sts.; Amen   Richard Baxter
        1683 Additions to the Poetical Fragments, pp. 62-
            69
            st. 29, ℓ. 1: "Christ who knows all his sheep"
        1855 American Plymouth Collection, with tune,
            No. 887

639.   My soul, let all thy noblest powers
            C. M.   8 sts.   Joseph Stennett
        1697 Hys. in Commem., No. VIII, p. 9
        No tune given but intended to be sung

640.   **My soul, my soul I feel, I feel is vexed
            **14 decasyllables   Barnaby Barnes
        **1595 A Divine Centurie of Spirituall Sonnets
            1815 Reprint, p. 30

641.   My soul, O god, doth now confess
            8. 8. 8. 8. 8. 8   2 sts.; Amen   William Hunnis
        1597 Humble Sutes bound with Seven Sobs of a

Sorrowfull Soule for Sinne, pp. 65-66
Tune in same volume   William Hunnis

642.   My soul, there is a country
             7. 6. 7. 6   20 ℓℓ.   Henry Vaughan
          1650 Silex Scintillans, p. 47
          *1867 The Peoples Hymnal, with tune, No. 526

643.   My soul! what's all this world to thee
             C. M.   9 sts.; Amen   John Austin
          1672 (1st ed. 1668) Devotions, No. XXVIII,
             pp. 246-247
          1701 Devot. ed. H., p. 327; tune p. 1, separate
             section

644.   My soul, why dost thou in my breast
             C. M. D.   8 sts.   George Wither
          1641 Hal. Pt. 1, No. CIX, pp. 213-215
          Suggested tune: Te Deum

645.   My soul, why dost thou linger so
             L. M. D.   9 sts.   George Wither
          1641 Hal. Pt. 1, No. LX, pp. 111-114
          Suggested tune: I love once

646.   My stock lies dead, and no increase
             8. 8. 8. 4   6 sts.   George Herbert
          1633 The Temple, pp. 52-53
          1742 Foundery, with tune, p. 14   St. John Tune

647.   My whole, though broken heart, O Lord
             C. M. D.   8 sts.   Richard Baxter
          1681 Poetical Fragments, pp. 81-83
             st. 2, ℓ. 1: "All that exceptions save I love"
             st. 3, ℓ. 1: "I know that thou wast willing
                first"
             st. 4, ℓ. 1: "Now it belongs not to my care"
             st. 5, ℓ. 1: "If death shall bruise this spring-
                ing seed"
             st. 6, ℓ. 1: "Would I long bear my heavy
                load"
             st. 7, ℓ. 1: "Christ leads me through no
                darker room"
             st. 7, ℓ. 5: "Come, Lord, when Grace hath
                made me meet"
             st. 8, ℓ. 1: "Then I shall end my sad com-
                plaints"
          Suggested tunes: Common Tunes

648. Mysterious truth! that the self same should be
        irreg.   15 ℓℓ.; Amen Jeremy Taylor
      1655 Festival Hymnes, appended to The Golden
           Grove, p. 148
      1754 C.H.C.G., Pt. I, No. 403, pp. 231-232
      L.M.   3 sts.
      Begins: "Strange truth, that the selfsame
        should be"
      Tune to be selected by meter from appended
      Table of Metres and Tunes

649. Nay, startle not to hear the rushing wind
        10.6.10.6.10   10 sts.   [Christopher Harvey]
      1673 The Synagogue, pp. 44-46
        st. 4, ℓ. 1: "Mock not, profane despisers of
        the spirit"
      1754 C.H.C.G., Pt. I: No. 381, p. 221
        10.10.6.8   5 sts.
      Begins: "Mock not profane despisers of the
        spirit"
      Tune to be selected by meter from appended
      Table of Metres and Tunes

650. **Never weather-beaten sail more willing bent to shore
        **13.13.15.13   2 sts.   Thomas Campion
      **1613 Two Bookes of Ayres, Bk. 1, No. XI
        **Tune in same volume   Thomas Campion
      1909 Campion's Works, p. 122

651. **Never yet could careless sleep
        **10 septisyllables   2 sts.   Joseph Beaumont
      **1643 Minor Poems, MS.
      1914 Reprint, p. 326

652. **Nigh to the fatal, and yet sov'reign wood
        **10.10.10.12   16 sts.   Seventeenth Century
      1754 C.H.C.G., Pt. I, No. 489, pp. 287-288
      Tune to be selected by meter from appended
      Table of Metres and Tunes

653. Night forbear; alas, our praise
        7.7.7.7   8 sts.; Amen   John Austin
      1672 (1st ed. 1668) Devotions, No. XXXIX,
           pp. 355-356
      1701 Devot. ed. H., p. 485; tune p. 11, separate
           section

654.   No bliss can so contenting prove
                  8. 8. 8. 8. 8. 8   14 sts.   George Wither
                1623 Hymns and Songs, No. LXXIX, p. 54
                  Tune in same volume: Song 9 Orlando Gibbons

655.   No doubt but she that had the grace
                  8. 8. 8. 8. 8. 8   5 sts.   George Wither
                1623 Hymns and Songs, No. L, p. 40
                  Tune in same volume: Song 9   Orlando Gibbons

656.   No earthly terror, Lord can make
                  C. M. D.   3 sts.   George Wither
                1641 Hal. Pt. 1, No. LXVI, pp. 124-125
                Suggested tune: Te Deum

657.   **No man hath seen thee, Father! but he who
                **10.10.10.10   10 sts.   Faithfull Teate
                1754 C. H. C. G., Pt. I, No. 385, pp. 224-225
                  Tune to be selected by meter from appended
                  Table of Metres and Tunes

658.   No outward mark we have to know
                  C. M. D.   4 sts.   George Wither
                1623 Hymns and Songs, No. LXXVIII, p. 53
                  Tune in same volume: Song 3   Orlando Gibbons

659.   No songs of triumph now be sung
                  C. M.   8 sts.
                1715 Divine Companion, 3rd ed.,
                    with tune, p. 18   Jer. Clarke

660.   No time, to trifle forth, in wast[e]
                  C. M. D.   6 sts.   George Wither
                1641 Hal Pt. 1, No. XL, pp. 64-66
                Suggested tune: Psalm 4

661.   Not in a mean degree
                  S. M. D.   6 sts.   George Wither
                1641 Hal. Pt. 3, No. XXX, pp. 414-416
                Suggested tune: Psalm 25

662.   Not in rich furniture, or fine array
                  10. 6. 6. 8. 10. 6   4 sts.   George Herbert
                  C. M.   4 sts.
                1633 The Temple, pp. 43-44
                  st. 2, ℓ . 1: "But by way of nourishment and
                  strength"

st. 5, ℓ . 1: "Give me my captive soul or
take"
1754 C. H. C. G., Pt. I, No. 357, pp. 213-214
8. 8. 8. 8. 8. 8   1 st.
Begins: "But by way of nourishment and
strength"
Tune to be selected by meter from appended
Table of Metres and Tunes
1754 C. H. C. G., Pt. I, No. 358
8. 7. 8. 7   4 sts.
Begins: "Give me my captive soul or take"
Tune to be selected by meter from appended
Table of Metres and Tunes

663.   Now are the times, these are the days
        C. M. D.   13 sts.   George Wither
        1641 Hal. Pt. 2, LIX, pp. 335-338
        Suggested tune: We praise Thee Oh God

664.   Now from the altar of our hearts
        C. M. D.   3 sts.   John Mason
        C. M.   1 st.
        1683 Spiritual Songs, No. XI, pp. 25-26
        st. 1, ℓ. 5: "Awake my love, awake my joy"
        st. 2, ℓ. 1: "Man's life's a book of history"
        No tune given but intended to be sung

665.   Now, glad and happy may I be
        L. M. D.   10 sts.   George Wither
        1641 Hal. Pt. 3, No. XLVI, pp. 446-449
        Suggested tune: I loved thee once

666.   Now, I perceive a God there is
        C. M. D.   5 sts.   George Wither
        1641 Hal. Pt. 3, No. LVIII, pp. 473-475
        Suggested tune: We praise thee God

667.   Now, in myself, I notice take
        8. 6. 8. 6. 4. 4. 6. 4. 4. 6   10 sts.   George Wither
        1641 Hal. Pt. 3, No. XXXVI, pp. 423-426
        No tune given but intended to be sung

668.   Now it belongs not to my care
        See: My whole though broken   Richard Baxter
              heart

669.   Now my dear friend is gone

6. 8. 6. 8. 4. 4. 6. 4. 4. 6   8 sts.   George Wither
1641 Hal. Pt. 1, No. LXXX, pp. 150-153
Suggested tune: In Sad and Ashie Weeds

670.   Now, my soul, the day is gone
        7. 6. 7. 6   9 sts.; Amen   John Austin
        1672 (1st ed. 1668) Devotions, No. VIII, pp. 76-
        77
        1671 Psalms and Hymns, with
        tune, pp. 74-75   John Playford

671.   Now that the sun hath veil'd his light
        irreg.   William Fuller
        1688 Harmonia Sacra, with tune,
        pp. 1-3   Henry Purcell

672.   Now that the Sun is at his height
        S. M. D.   4 sts.   George Wither
        1641 Hal. Pt. 1, No. XIII, pp. 19-20
        Suggested tunes: Psalms 16 or 18

673.   Now that this morning here we are
        L. M.   5 sts.
        1688 St. Martin's, p. 84
        Tune in same volume: Psalm 100

674.   Now, that thou and I must part
        7. 7. 7. 7. 7. 7. 7. 7   5 sts.   George Wither
        1641 Hal. Pt. 3, No. XIX, pp. 386-388
        No tune given but intended to be sung

675.   Now the cheerful day is past
        7. 7. 7. 7. D.   5 sts.   George Wither
        1641 Hal. Pt. 1, No. XVIII, pp. 26-27
        No tune given but intended to be sung

676.   Now the earth begins to mourn
        7. 7. 7. 7. 7. 7   8 sts.   George Wither
        1641 Hal. Pt. 2, pp. 270-272
        No tune given but intended to be sung

677.   Now, the glories of the year
        L. M. D.   6 sts.   George Wither
        1641 Hal. Pt. 2, No. XX, pp. 268-269
        No tune given but intended to be sung

678.   O beauteous God, uncircumscribed treasure

irreg.   32 *ℓℓ*.; Allelujah; Amen   Jeremy Taylor
1655 Festival Hymnes appended to The Golden
Grove, pp. 157-158

679.   O blessed Lord, O blessed Lord
C. M. D.   4 sts.
1715 The Divine Companion, 3rd
ed., with tune, pp. 28-30   Dr. Turner

680.   O blessed Lord! why dost thou love
See: O Lord my saviour and support

681.   *O blessed Saviour is thy love
See: My blessed Saviour is   Joseph Stennett
thy love

682.   O blessed well of love, O flower of grace
See: Love, lift me up upon   Edmund Spenser
thy golden wings

683.   **O bless'd be God for ever blest
**C. M.   42 sts.   [Sixteenth Century]
1754 C. H. C. G., Pt. I, No. 423, pp. 243-244
Tune to be selected by meter from appended
Table of Metres and Tunes

684.   O book! infinite sweetness! let my heart
10.10.10.10   3 sts.   George Herbert
10.10
1633 The Temple, p. 50

685.   O Christ! this day thy flesh did bleed
See: This day, O Christ!   George Wither
thy flesh

686.   O come away
4.4.8.4.4.8   13 sts.   Henry Vaughan
1655 Silex Scintillans, Pt. II, pp. 72-74

687.   No entry.

688.   O day of God most calm, most bright
See: Blest day of God   John Mason

689.   O day most calm, most bright
        6. 8. 8. 8. 8. 8. 6   9 sts.   George Herbert
        1633 The Temple, pp. 66-68
           st. 5, ℓ. 1: "The Sundaies of man's life"
           *Sung during Herbert's lifetime
        *1697 Select Hymns from Mr. Herbert's Temple,
           with tune
        1754 C. H. C. G., Pt. I, No. 355, p. 213
           8. 8. 8. 8. 8. 8   3 sts.
           Begins: "The sev'ral Sundays of man's life"
           Tune to be selected by meter from appended
           Table of Metres and Tunes

690.   **O glorious crown! more precious many ways
           **14 decasyllables   Barnaby Barnes
        **1595 A Divine Centurie of Spirituall Sonnets
        1815 Reprint, p. 36

691.   O glorious, dear, dread Trinity
           irreg.   4 sts.   Lancelot Addison
        1699 Devotional Poems, pp. 43-44

692.   O God, be thou my living rock
           8. 8. 8. 8. 8. 8   John Quarles
        1663 Divine Meditations... With... Divine Ejacula-
           tions, p. 136

693.   O God, how poor a thing is man
           8. 8. 8. 8. 8. 8   John Quarles
        1663 Divine Meditations... With... Divine Ejacula-
           tions, p. 159

694.   O God of grace, who hath restored
           S. M. D.   4 sts.   John Mason
           C. M.   1 st.
        1683 Spiritual Songs, No. XXV, pp. 54-55
           No tune given but intended to be sung

695.   O God of love
           C. M.   7 sts.
        1715 Divine Companion, 3rd ed., with
           tune, pp. 145-146   B. R.

696.   O God, remit thy peoples sin
           8. 8. 8. 8. 8. 8   John Quarles
        1663 Divine Meditations... With... Divine Ejacula-
           tions, p. 153

697.   O God, that guides the cheerful sun
         L. M. D.
         8. 8   Chorus
         1588 Psalms, Sonets, and Songs,
              with tune, No. 28   William Byrd

698.   O God, the malice of my foes
         8. 8. 8. 8. 8. 8   John Quarles
         1663 Divine Meditations... With... Divine Ejacula-
              tions, p. 145

699.   O God, the mountains and the seas
         8. 8. 8. 8. 8. 8   John Quarles
         1663 Divine Meditations... With... Divine Ejacula-
              tions, p. 163

700.   O God, the Sion of my soul
         8. 8. 8. 8. 8. 8   John Quarles
         1663 Divine Meditations... With... Divine Ejacula-
              tions, p. 151

701.   O God thy law's a field, in which
         8. 8. 8. 8. 8. 8   John Quarles
         1663 Divine Meditations... With... Divine Ejacula-
              tions, p. 164

702.   O God to whom thy thoughts direct
         8. 8. 8. 8. 8. 8   John Quarles
         1663 Divine Meditations... With... Divine Ejacula-
              tions, p. 165

703.   O God, whose dreadful voice, like thunder
         8. 8. 8. 8. 8. 8   John Quarles
         1663 Divine Meditations... With... Divine Ejacula-
              tions, p. 151

704.   O God, whose judgments are severe
         8. 8. 8. 8. 8. 8   John Quarles
         1663 Divine Meditations... With... Divine Ejacula-
              tions, p. 134

705.   **O gracious God and heavenly Father dear
             **10. 10. 10. 10   21 sts.   W. A.
         **1579 Three Collections of English Poetry
         1845 Farr, Vol. 2, p. 508

706.   **O gracious God, O Saviour sweet

      **C. M.   9 sts.   Anonymous
     1890 Palgrave, p. 16

707. **O heavenly God, O Father dear
        **C. M.   12 sts.   Walter Devereux
        **Sloane MSS., British Mus., (Earl of Essex)
        1896, p. 52
     1814 Egerton Brydges, ed., Excerpta Tudoriana,
        pp. 14-16
     1591 The Second Booke, with   Wm. Damon
        music, Cantus, p. 46; Quintus, p. 47

708.   O holy, blessed, glorious three
        8. 8. 8   3 sts.   Henry Vaughan
     1655 Silex Scintillans, Pt. II, p. 17

709.   O holy blessed, glorious Trinity
        10. 10. 10. 4   12 sts.   Ben. Johnson [sic.]
     1640 Underwoods, pp. 163-164

710.   O holy, holy, holy Lord
        C. M.   4 sts.   Dryden
     1903 Hymns of the Christian Centuries, p. 133

711.   O holy sacrament this day
        See: "A holy sacrament this   George Wither
        day"

712.   **O holy spirit our comforter
        **8. 8. 8. 9. 10. 9   5 sts.   Unknown
    **c. 1539 Goostly Psalmes and Spirituall Songs
        **Tune in same volume
     1846 Remains of Myles Coverdale, pp. 541-542

713.   Oh! how my mind is gravel'd! Not a thought
        18 decasyllables   [Christopher Harvey]
     1640 The Synagogue, pp. 12-13

714.   O how uneasy does it seem
        irreg.   4 sts.   Lancelot Addison
     1699 Devotional Poems, pp. 39-40

715.   O I'm all ecstacy, and love, and flame
        10. 10. 10. 10   5 sts.   Lancelot Addison
        10. 10. 10. 10. 10. 10 2 sts.
     1699 Devotional Poems, pp. 56-58

716.   O Jesu, be not long away
         C. M.   3 sts.   William Hunnis
         1597 A Handfull of Honisuckles, bound with Seven
              Sobs of a Sorrowfull Soule for Sinne,
              pp. 10-11
         Tune in same volume   William Hunnis

717.   O Jesu Christ, in all things now
         C. M.   3 sts.; Amen   William Hunnis
         1597 A Handfull of Honisuckles, bound with Seven
              Sobs of a Sorrowfull Soule for Sinne, pp. 4-
              5
         Tune in same volume   William Hunnis

718.   O Jesu Christ, that hast me made
         C. M.   3 sts.; Amen   William Hunnis
         1597 A Handfull of Honisuckles, bound with Seven
              Sobs of a Sorrowfull Soule for Sinne, p. 9
         Tune in same volume   William Hunnis

719.   O Jesu Christ, under whose power
         C. M.   3 sts.; Amen   William Hunnis
         1597 A Handfull of Honisuckles, bound with Seven
              Sobs of a Sorrowfull Soule for Sinne, p. 8
         Tune in same volume   William Hunnis

720.   O Jesu, comfort mine exile
         C. M.   3 sts.; Amen   William Hunnis
         1597 A Handfull of Honisuckles, bound with Seven
              Sobs of a Sorrowfull Soule for Sinne, pp. 8-
              9
         Tune in same volume   William Hunnis

721.   O Jesu dear, do thou with me
         C. M.   3 sts.; Amen   William Hunnis
         1597 A Handfull of Honisuckles, bound with Seven
              Sobs of a Sorrowfull Soule for Sinne, p. 2
         Tune in same volume   William Hunnis

722.   O Jesu dear, give me thy grace
         C. M.   3 sts.; Amen   William Hunnis
         1597 A Handfull of Honisuckles, bound with Seven
              Sobs of a Sorrowfull Soule for Sinne, p. 4
         Tune in same volume   William Hunnis

723.   O Jesu, grant I may resign
         C. M.   3 sts.; Amen   William Hunnis

1597 A Handfull of Honisuckles, bound with Seven
   Sobs of a Sorrowfull Soule for Sinne, p. 6
Tune in same volume   William Hunnis

724.   O Jesu, here in earth we live
        C. M.   3 sts. ; Amen   William Hunnis
        1597 A Handfull of Honisuckles, bound with Seven
           Sobs of a Sorrowfull Soule for Sinne, p. 8
        Tune in same volume   William Hunnis

725.   O Jesu, if thou do withdraw
        C. M.   3 sts. ; Amen   William Hunnis
        1597 A Handfull of Honisuckles, bound with Seven
           Sobs of a Sorrowfull Soule for Sinne, p. 3
        Tune in same volume   William Hunnis

726.   O Jesu, king of glory great
        C. M.   3 sts. ; Amen   William Hunnis
        1597 A Handfull of Honisuckles, bound with Seven
           Sobs of a Sorrowfull Soule for Sinne, pp. 5-
           6
        Tune in same volume   William Hunnis

727.   O Jesu, let me reach my hand to thee
        irreg.   4 sts.   Lancelot Addison
        1699 Devotional Poems, pp. 77-78

728.   O Jesu, many times I pray
        C. M.   3 sts.; Amen   William Hunnis
        1597 A Handfull of Honisuckles, bound with Seven
           Sobs of a Sorrowfull Soule for Sinne, p. 10
        Tune in same volume   William Hunnis

729.   O Jesu meek, grant that I may
        C. M.   3 sts. ; Amen   William Hunnis
        1597 A Handfull of Honisuckles, bound with Seven
           Sobs of a Sorrowfull Soule for Sinne, p. 3
        Tune in same volume   William Hunnis

730.   O Jesu meek, O Jesu sweet
        C. M.   3 sts. ; Amen   William Hunnis
        1597 A Handfull of Honisuckles, bound with Seven
           Sobs of a Sorrowfull Soule for Sinne, pp. 1-
           2
        Tune in same volume   William Hunnis

731.   O Jesu mild, thine ear bow down

      C. M.   3 sts.; Amen   William Hunnis
    1597 A Handfull of Honisuckles, bound with Seven
       Sobs of a Sorrowfull Soule for Sinne, p. 11
    Tune in same volume   William Hunnis

732.   O Jesu, oft it grieveth me
      C. M.   3 sts.; Amen   William Hunnis
    1597 A Handfull of Honisuckles, bound with Seven
       Sobs of a Sorrowfull Soule for Sinne, p. 6
    Tune in same volume   William Hunnis

733.   O Jesu, shut not up my soul
      C. M.   3 sts.; Amen   William Hunnis
    1597 A Handfull of Honisuckles, bound with Seven
       Sobs of a Sorrowfull Soule for Sinne, p. 12
    Tune in same volume   William Hunnis

734.   O Jesu, sweet, a little thing
      C. M.   3 sts.; Amen   William Hunnis
    1597 A Handfull of Honisuckles, bound with Seven
       Sobs of a Sorrowfull Soule for Sinne, p. 4
    Tune in same volume   William Hunnis

735.   O Jesu sweet, for heavenly things
      C. M.   3 sts.; Amen   William Hunnis
    1597 A Handfull of Honisuckles, bound with Seven
       Sobs of a Sorrowfull Soule for Sinne, pp. 9-
       10
    Tune in same volume   William Hunnis

736.   O Jesu sweet, give me an heart
      C. M.   3 sts.; Amen   William Hunnis
    1597 A Handfull of Honisuckles, bound with Seven
       Sobs of a Sorrowfull Soule for Sinne, p. 12
    Tune in same volume   William Hunnis

737.   O Jesu sweet, grant that thy grace
      C. M.   3 sts.; Amen   William Hunnis
    1597 A Handfull of Honisuckles, bound with Seven
       Sobs of a Sorrowfull Soule for Sinne, p. 2
    Tune in same volume   William Hunnis

738.   O Jesu sweet, I know I am
      C. M.   3 sts.; Amen   William Hunnis
    1597 A Handfull of Honisuckles, bound with Seven
       Sobs of a Sorrowfull Soule for Sinne, p. 7
    Tune in same volume   William Hunnis

739.   O Jesu sweet, with mercy now
            C. M.   3 sts.; Amen   William Hunnis
        1597 A Handfull of Honisuckles, bound with Seven
            Sobs of a Sorrowfull Soule for Sinne, pp. 11-
            12
        Tune in same volume   William Hunnis

740.   O Jesu, thou my glory art
            C. M.   3 sts.; Amen   William Hunnis
        1597 A Handfull of Honisuckles, bound with Seven
            Sobs of a Sorrowfull Soule for Sinne, p. 7
        Tune in same volume   William Hunnis

741.   O Jesu, who shall give me wings
            C. M.   3 sts.; Amen   William Hunnis
        1597 A Handfull of Honisuckles, bound with Seven
            Sobs of a Sorrowfull Soule for Sinne, p. 5
        Tune in same volume   William Hunnis

742.   *O King of Kings, before whose throne
          *1655 Divine Meditations upon   John Quarles
              Several Subjects
          *1889 Hymns for the Church of England

743.   O Lord, behold a wretched one
            L. M.   6 sts.   [Thomas Shepherd]
        1693 Penetential Cries, No. XX, p. 31
        Suggested tune: Psalm 100

744.   O Lord, how shall we frame a song
            C. M.   8 sts.   Joseph Stennett
        1697 Hys. in Commem., No. XVIII, p. 21
        No tune given but intended to be sung

745.   O Lord I fain would sing thy praise
            L. M. D.   8 sts.   George Wither
        1641 Hal. Pt. 1, No. XXI, pp. 30-33
        Suggested tune: Psalm 100

746.   O Lord! in sorrow and distress
            8. 6. 8. 6   George Wither
            3   3
            3   3   6 sts.
            2   2
            2   2
            2   2
        1641 Hal. Pt. 1, No. XCIII, pp. 180-182
        No tune given but intended to be sung

747.   O Lord in thee is all my trust
        L. M. D.   3 sts.   Unknown
        c. 1559 The First Parte of the Booke of Psalmes,
            unpaged
        Tune in same volume   Unknown

748.   **O Lord! increase in me true faith and love
        **14 decasyllables   Barnaby Barnes
        **1595 A Divine Centurie of Spirituall Sonnets
        1815 Reprint, p. 23

749.   O Lord my God, I wandered have
        C. M.   5 sts.; Amen   William Hunnis
        1597 A Handfull of Honisuckles, bound with Seven
            Sobs of a Sorrowfull Soule for Sinne, p. 14
        Tune in same volume   William Hunnis

750.   O Lord my judgement's dark, and blind
        8. 8. 8. 8. 8. 8   John Quarles
        1663 Divine Meditations... With... Divine Ejacula-
            tions, p. 173

751.   O Lord my Saviour and support
        C. M.   9 sts.
        1671 Psalms and Hymns, with
            tune, pp. 26-27   John Playford
        st. 2, ℓ. 1: "O blessed Lord! why dost thou
            love"

752.   **O Lord my sins doth overcharge thy breast
        **6 decasyllables 7 sts.   Robert Southwell
        **1634 St. Peter's Complaint, pp. 90-91
        1856 Reprint

753.   O Lord, now I the favor have
        C. M.   7 sts.
        1715 Divine Companion, 3rd ed.
            with tune, pp. 65-66   Doctor Crofts

754.   O Lord, O Lord, what have I done
        C. M. D.   4 sts.   [John Mason]
        1693 Penetential Cries, No. I
        No tune given but intended to be sung

755.   O Lord of whom I do depend
        C. M. D.   7 sts.   M. [John Marckant]
        c. 1559 The First Parte of the Booke of Psalmes,
            unpaged

Tune in same volume   Unknown

756.   O Lord, this night who hast me kept
        C. M.   5 sts.; Amen   William Hunnis
        1597 A Handfull of Honisuckles, bound with Seven
             Sobs of a Sorrowfull Soule for Sinne, p. 15
        Tune in same volume   William Hunnis

757.   O Lord, thou dost a broken heart
        C. M.   9 sts.   Joseph Stennett
        1697 Hys. in Commem., No. XXVIII, p. 36
        No tune given but intended to be sung

758.   O Lord, turn not away thy face
        C. M. D.   4 sts.   John Marckant
        C. M.   1 st.; Amen
        c.1559 The First Parte of the Booke of Psalmes,
              pp. 19-21
        Tune in same volume   Unknown

759.   O Lord! we magnify thy might
        L. M. D.   4 sts.   George Wither
        1641 Hal. Pt. 1, No. LXXV, pp. 138-140
        Suggested tune: 10 Com.

760.   *O Lord when near the appointed hour
        *1721 Hymns for all the Festivals   Thomas Ken
              of the Year

761.   O Lord whose mercies, and whose paths
        8. 8. 8. 8. 8. 8   John Quarles
        1663 Divine Meditations... With... Divine Ejacula-
             tions, p. 161

762.   *O make us apt to seek, and quick to find
        See: I sought thee round   Thomas Heywood
              about

763.   **O mercy! mercy! which much greater is
        **14 decasyllables   Barnaby Barnes
        **1595 A Divine Centurie of Spirituall Sonnets
        1815 Reprint, p. 33

764.   **O mighty God, who for us men
        **C. M. D.   4 sts.   Humphrey Gifford
        1890 Palgrave, p. 11

765.   O my chief good
        4. 8. 8. 4   5 sts.   George Herbert
        8. 8. 8. 8   3 sts.
        1633 The Temple, pp. 30-31
        1754 C. H. C. G., Pt. I, No. 359, p. 214
        L. M.   1 st.
        4. 8. 8. 4   2 sts.
        Tune to be selected by meter from appended
        Table of Metres and Tunes

766.   O my chief good
        4.4.4.8.4.4.4.4.8.4.4.4.4.8 (4 sts.) Henry Vaughan
        1650 Silex Scintillans, pp. 47-49

767.   O my life, my all, my dear
        See: My love, my life, my   Lancelot Addison
        dear, my all

768.   O my God! what helpeth less
        7. 7. 7. 7. 7. 7. 7. 7   5 sts.   George Wither
        1641 Hal. Pt. 3, No. XXXIII, pp. 418-419
        No tune given but intended to be sung

769.   O pleasant spot! O place of rest
        L. M.   7 sts.   Robert Southwell
        1634 Maeoniae, pp. 134-135

770.   O praise the Lord, praise him, praise him
        C. M. D.   8 sts.   John Mason
        C. M.   1 st.
        1683 Spiritual Songs, No. XVIII, pp. 40-42
        (No. XXXI, taken from Psalms, used the same
        first line but continued differently)
        No tune given but intended to be sung

771.   *O purify my soul from stain
      *1721 Hymns for all the Festivals   Thomas Ken
        of the Year

772.   O sacred spirit, within my soul repeat
        10.10.10.10   4 sts.   Seventeenth Century
        1754 C. H. C. G., Pt. I, No. 500, p. 292
        Tune to be selected by meter from appended
        Table of Metres and Tunes

773.   O save us then
        irreg.   14 ℓℓ.   Richard Crashaw

1648 Steps to the Temple, p. 13
1754 C. H. C. G., Pt. I, No. 395, p. 229
irreg.   10 ℓℓ.
Tune to be selected by meter from appended
Table of Metres and Tunes

774.   O sing the glories of our Lord
        See: Come ravisht souls   Thomas Pestel

775.   **O, sun and moon! the days and evening lights
           **14 decasyllables   Barnaby Barnes
        **1595 A Divine Centurie of Spirituall Sonnets
        1815 Reprint, p. 24

776.   O that I had an angel's tongue
           C. M. D.   9 sts.   John Mason
        1683 Spiritual Songs, No. XIV, pp. 30-33
        No tune given but intended to be sung

777.   O that it may one day be said by thee
           15 decasyllables   Seventeenth Century
        1754 C. H. C. G., Pt. I, No. 515, pp. 297-298
        Tune to be selected by meter from appended
        Table of Metres and Tunes

778.   O that mine eyes would melt into a flood
           irreg.   16 ℓℓ.
        1688 Harmonia Sacra, pp. 66-67   John Blow

779.   O that my soul as prosperous were
           See: O that my soul   [Thomas Shepherd]
                 was now as fair

780.   O that my soul was now as fair
           C. M. D.   4 sts.   [Thomas Shepherd]
           C. M.   1 st.
        1693 Penetential Cries, No. XVI, p. 20
        No tune given but intended to be sung

781.   *O that thou wouldst hide me in the grave
           *1634-35 Emblems, Bk. iii,   Francis Quarles
              pp. 75-76

782.   O these wakeful wounds of thine
           7. 7. 7. 8   5 sts.   Richard Crashaw
        1646 Steps to the Temple, pp. 21-22
        1754 C. H. C. G., Pt. I, No. 398, p. 230

7.7.7.7   3 sts.
Tune to be selected by meter from appended
Table of Metres and Tunes

783.   **O thou eternal spright! cleave ope the sky
          **9 decasyllables   Henry More
       **1640 Psychozoia
       1871 Songs of the spirit, p. 307

784.   O thou great power, in whom I move
          8. 8. 8. 8. 8. 8   3 sts.   Sir Henry Wotton
       1651 Reliquiae Wottonianae, p. 515

785.   O thou that sit'st in heaven, and seest
          8. 8. 8. 8. 8. 8   John Quarles
       1663 Divine Meditations... With... Divine Ejacula-
          tions, p. 161
       1852 Hys. for Christian Ch. and Hm., No. 436
       Choice of tunes from other books

786.   O thou, within whose tender breast
          8. 8. 8. 8. 8. 8   John Quarles
       1663 Divine Meditations... With... Divine Ejacula-
          tions, p. 159

787.   O thou who taught'st the blind man's night
          See: Full of mercy, full of   Jeremy Taylor
          love

788.   O thou, whose mercy did begin
          8. 8. 8. 8. 8. 8   John Quarles
       1663 Divine Meditations... With... Divine Ejacula-
          tions, p. 151

789.   **O thou whose scales the mountains weigh
          **L. M. D.   3 sts.   John Mason
       1772 Tate and Brady, No. XLII
       Tune in same volume

790.   *O throw away thy rod
          See: Throw away thy rod   Herbert/Wesley

791.   **O vile and inconsid'rate man
          **C. M.   28 sts.   [Sixteenth Century]
       1754 C. H. C. G., Pt. I, No. 424, pp. 245-246
       Tune to be selected by meter from appended
          Table of Metres and Tunes

792.   O what a war is in my soul
         C. M. D.   3 sts.   [Thomas Shepherd]
         C. M.   1 st.
         1693 Penetential Cries, No. XVII, p. 21
         No tune given but intended to be sung

793.   **O what great comfort is it, to give praise
         **14 decasyllables   Barnaby Barnes
       **1595 A Divine Centurie of Spirituall Sonnets
         1815 Reprint, p. 23

794.   **O what is man, great Maker of mankind
         **10.10.10.10   5 sts.   Sir John Davies
       **1599 The Soul of Man
         1838 Hendee, No. 510   3 sts.
         No tune given but intended to be sung

795.   O what is't Lord, that you would have me do
         See: Adieu, dear Lord, if   Lancelot Addison
            you'll ascend from me

796.   O when my God, my glory brings
         C. M.   4 sts.   Henry Vaughan
         1655 Silex Scintillans, Pt. II, p. 61

797.   Of all those judgements which thy word
         L. M. D.   8 sts.   George Wither
         1641 Hal. Pt. 1, No. LXXIII, pp. 134-137
         Suggested tune: Psalm 51

798.   On all the earth thy spirit shower
         See: When Christ His body up   Henry More
            had borne

799.   **On thee, my sure foundation
         **C. M.   3 sts.   [Sixteenth Century]
         1754 C. H. C. G., Pt. I, No. 429, p. 249
         Tune to be selected by meter from appended
         Table of Metres and Tunes

800.   On those great waters now I am
         C. M. D.   5 sts.   George Wither
         1641 Hal. Pt. 1, No. XXV, pp. 39-41
         Suggested tune: Psalm 48

801.   Open thine eyes, my soul, and see
         L. M.   7 sts.; Amen   John Austin

1672 (1st ed. 1668) Devotions, No. XIII, p. 110
1671 Psalms and Hymns, with tune, pp. 58-59
  **Altered version begins: John Playford
  "Awake, my soul awake, and see"

802.   Others may tell of famous things
            L. M.   11 sts.   Joseph Stennett
        1697 Hys. in Commem., No. XXXVII, p. 49
        Suggested tune: Psalm 100

803.   **Our gold, rich king of poverty
                **irreg.   12 ℓ ℓ.   Joseph Beaumont
        **c.1643 Minor Poems, MS.
            **Marked: To a Base and 2 Trebles
        1914 Reprint, p. 135

804.   Our hearts, Oh blessed God incline
            L. M. D.   3 sts.   George Wither
        1623 Hymns and Songs, No. LII, p. 41
        Tune in same volume: Song   Orlando Gibbons
            44

805.   Our Lord a banquet has prepared
            L. M.   7 sts.   Joseph Stennett
        1697 Hys. in Commem., No. XXIII, p. 29
        Suggested tune: Psalm 100

806.   Our voice how should we raise!
            6.6.6.6.4.8.4   8 sts.   George Wither
        1641 Hal. Pt. 1, No. LII, pp. 87-89
        Suggested tune: Psalm 148

807.   Philosophers have measur'd mountains
            8.10.10.8.10.10   3 sts.   George Herbert
        1633 The Temple, p. 29
            st. 2, ℓ. 1:   "Who would know sin let him re-
                pair"
        1754 C. H. C. G., Pt. I, No. 353, p. 212
            8.8.8.8.8.8
        Begins: "Who would know sin let him repair"
        Tune to be selected by meter from appended
            Table of Metres and Tunes

808.   Plung'd in grief and in distress
            11 septisyllables 12 sts.   George Wither
        1641 Hal. Pt. 2, No. X, pp. 243-248
        No tune given but intended to be sung

809.   Poor soul, the centre of my sinful earth
        14 decasyllables   Wm. Shakespeare
        1609 Sonnets, No. 146
        1925 Songs of Praise, with tune, No. 622

810.   Prepare for songs; He's come, He's come
        irreg.   29 ℓℓ.   Robert Herrick
        1647 Noble Numbers, p. 32-33 "Sung to the King
            in the Presence at White Hall"
        Note at the end that it was "Composed by
            M. Henry Lawes" but tune not given

811.   Prevent, Lord, by thy grace
        S. M. D.   7 sts.   George Wither
        1641 Hal. Pt. 3, No. XXXIX, pp. 432-436
        Suggested tune: Psalm 25

812.   Prostrate, O Lord, I lie
        6. 7. 8. 7. 6. 6. 8. 6   3 sts.
        1588 Psalms, Sonets and Songs,
            with tune, No. 27   William Byrd

813.   Pure and spotless was the maid
        irreg.   23 ℓℓ.; Amen Jeremy Taylor
        1655 Festival Hymnes appended to The Golden
            Grove, pp. 160-161

814.   **Purge thou my guilty soul, sweet gracious Lord!
        **14 decasyllables   Barnaby Barnes
        **1595 A Divine Centurie of Spirituall Sonnets
        1815 Reprint, p. 39

815.   **Put not your trust in fading earth
        **C. M.   12 sts.   Ann Dowriche
        1845 Farr Vol. 2, p. 359

816.   Quite lost, are now mine ayerie joys
        10 octosyllables   5 sts.   George Wither
        1641 Hal. Pt. 3, No. XIII, pp. 376-378
        Suggested tune: The Lamentation

817.   Rejoice not without fear, my heart
        10 octosyllables   George Wither
        1641 Hal. Pt. 3, No. XXVIII, pp. 408-410
        Suggested tune: The Lamentation

818.   **Relieve my soul with thy dear mercies balms

               **14 decasyllables   Barnaby Barnes
          **1595 A Divine Centurie of Spirituall Sonnets
          1815 Reprint, p. 47

819.   Remember death: for, now my tongue
          8. 8. 8. 8. 8. 8   6 sts.   George Wither
          1641 Hal. Pt. 1, No. LVI, pp. 98-100
          No tune given but intended to be sung

820.   **Remember how, beside the bands
          **8. 8. 8. 8. 10. 10   [Sixteenth Century]
          1754 C. H. C. G. , Pt. I, No. 427, p. 249
          Tune to be selected by meter from appended
          Table of Metres and Tunes

821.   Renowned men their herds to keep
          10 octosyllables   7 sts.   George Wither
          1641 Hal. Pt. 3, No. XLI, pp. 436-438
          Suggested tune: The Lamentation

822.   Return, my soul, enjoy thy rest
          See: Another six days   Joseph Stennett

823.   Rich gifts, and graces manifold
          L. M. D.   3 sts.   George Wither
          1641 Hal. Pt. 2, No. L, pp. 321-322
          Suggested tune: 10 Com.

824.   **Ride on the glory, on the morning's wings
          **14 decasyllables   Barnaby Barnes
          **1595 A Divine Centurie of Spirituall Sonnets
          1815 Reprint, p. 40

825.   Ring out, ye crystal spheres!
          See: "This is the month, and   John Milton
            this the happy morn"

826.   Rise heart; thy Lord is risen, sing his praise
          10. 4. 10. 4. 10. 4 3 sts.   George Herbert
          8. 8. 8. 8   3 sts.
          1633 The Temple, p. 33
          st. 4, ℓ . 1: "I got me flowers to straw thy
            way"
          1852 Hys. for Christian Ch. and Hm. , 9th ed. ,
            No. 644
          Choice of tunes from other books

827.   Rise, oh my soul, with thy desires to heaven
                 10.10.10.10.10.10   3 sts.   Sir Henry Wotton
            1651 Reliquiae Wottonianae, p. 537
            1708 Lyra Davidica, with tune, p. 38

828.   Rise royal Sion! rise and sing
                 8. 8. 8. 8. 8. 8   9 sts.; Amen   John Austin
            1672 (1st ed. 1668) Devotions, No. XVII, pp.
                 144-146
            1701 Devot. ed. H., p. 187; tune p. 4, separate
                 section

829.   Rise, royal Sion! rise and sing
                 8. 8. 8. 8. 8. 8   14 sts.   Richard Crashaw
            1648 Steps to the Temple, pp. 76-78

830.   Rise, thou first and fairest morning
                 8. 8. 8. 8   9 sts.   Richard Crashaw
                 10.10
            1646 Steps to the Temple, pp. 94-95

831.   Rivers run, and springs each one
                 See: Canst be idle? canst   George Herbert
                 thou play

832.   **Sacred, dear Father of all things created
                 *10.10.10.10.6.10.10   8 sts. Barnaby Barnes
            **1595 A Divine Centurie of Spirituall Sonnets
                 Was marked "Hymne"
            1815 Reprint, pp. 52-53

833.   **Sacred director of divine Sion
                 **14 decasyllables   Barnaby Barnes
            **1595 A Divine Centurie of Spirituall Sonnets
                 1815 Reprint, p. 51

834.   **Sacred Redeemer! let my prayers pierce
                 **14 decasyllables   Barnaby Barnes
            **1595 A Divine Centurie of Spirituall Sonnets
                 1815 Reprint, p. 2

835.   Said I not so, that I would sin no more
                 irreg.   5 sts.   [Christopher Harvey]
            1640 The Synagogue, pp. 11-12

836.   Said (not causless) it hath been
                 7. 7. 7. 7. 7. 7. 7. 7   8 sts.   George Wither

1641 Hal. Pt. 3, No. LI, pp. 457-459
No tune given but intended to be sung

837.   *Saviour, if thy precious love
          See: Sweetest Saviour, if   Herbert/Wesley
          my soul

838.   **Say, bold and daring mind
            **irreg.   200 ℓ ℓ .   Seventeenth Century
          1754 C. H. C. G. , Pt. I, No. 487, pp. 283-286
          Tune to be selected by meter from appended
          Table of Metres and Tunes

839.   See brethren, what a pleasing bliss
            8. 8. 8. 8. 8. 8. 6. 6. 6. 6   3 sts.   George Wither
          1641 Hal. Pt. 2, No. XV, pp. 257-259
          Suggested tune: Psalm 133

840.   **See how the willing converts trace
            **L. M.   4 sts.   Joseph Stennett
          1804 Rippon, No. CCCCL
          Suggested tune: Old Hundred etc.

841.   See, see, the sky from storms is clear
            L. M. D.   7 sts.   George Wither
          1641 Hal. Pt. 1, No. XXVII, pp. 44-46
          Suggested tune: Psalm 100

842.   **See sinful soul thy saviour's suffering see
            **10. 10. 10. 10   3 sts.   W. Stroud
          1671 Psalms and Hymns, with
            tune, p. 89   John Playford

843.   **Seek the Lord, and in his ways persevere
            **10. 8. 6. 11   4 sts.   Thomas Campion
          **1613 Two Bookes of Ayres, Bk. I, No. 18
            **Tune in same volume   Thomas Campion
          1909 Campion's Works, p. 126

844.   Shall frost and snow give praise to thee
            8. 8. 8. 8. 8. 8   John Quarles
          1663 Divine Meditations... With... Divine Ejacula-
            tions, p. 174

845.   **Shall I the image of my God deface
            **7 decasyllables   Seventeenth Century
          1754 C. H. C. G. , Pt. I, No. 521, p. 299

Tune to be selected by meter from appended
Table of Metres and Tunes

846.   Shall mountain, desert, beast, and tree
           8. 8. 8. 8. 8. 8   John Quarles
        1663 Divine Meditations... With... Divine Ejacula-
        tions, p. 136

847.   Since all of us, near kinsmen be
           C. M. D.   5 sts.   George Wither
        1641 Hal. Pt. 2, No. XXVII, pp. 280-281
        Suggested tune: Psalm 4

848.   Since, by election, I am sent
           8. 8. 8. 8. 8. 8   7 sts.   George Wither
        1641 Hal. Pt. 3, No. VI, pp. 360-362
        Suggested tune: The Lords Prayer

849.   Since in a land not barren still
           8. 8. 8   6 sts.   Henry Vaughan
        1650 Silex Scintillans, p. 88

850.   Since, Lord thou hast well pleased been
           C. M. D.   2 sts.   George Wither
        1641 Hal. Pt. 1, No. XII, p. 18
        Suggested tunes: Psalm 16 or 18

851.   Since now, my babe, of sleep possest
           C. M. D.   7 sts.   George Wither
        1641 Hal. Pt. 1, No. LI, pp. 85-87
        Suggested tunes: Psalm 1 or Te Deum

852.   Since they in singing, take delight
           L. M. D.   13 sts.   George Wither
        1641 Hal. Pt. 3, No. XXI, pp. 390-393
        Suggested tune: I loved thee once

853.   Since thou hast added, now, O God
           8. 8. 8. 8. 8. 8   6 sts.   George Wither
        1641 Hal. Pt. 1, No. V, pp. 8-10
        Suggested tune: The Pater Noster

854.   Since thou hast Lord, appointed so
           L. M. D.   2 sts.   George Wither
        1641 Hal. Pt. 1, No. VIII, pp. 12-13
        Suggested tune: The 10 Com.

855.   Sing Hallelujah to our Lord
            C. M.   7 sts.   Joseph Stennett
        1697 Hys. in Commem., No. XIX, p. 23
        No tune given but intended to be sung

856.   Sing, my soul, to God thy Lord
            7. 7. 7. 7. 7. 7. 7   (17 sts.; Amen)Nicholas Breton
        1601 The Ravished Soul, pp. 7-11

857.   Sing to Jehovah a new song
            C. M.   9 sts.   Joseph Stennett
        1697 Hys in Commem., No. XXIV, p. 30
        No tune given but intended to be sung

858.   Sion, the glory of all the earth
            8. 8. 8. 8. 8. 8   John Quarles
        1663 Divine Meditations... With... Divine Ejacula-
             tions, p. 154

859.   Six days, Oh Lord, the world to make
            L. M. D.   3 sts.   George Wither
        1623 Hymns and Songs, No. LX, p. 46
        Tune in same volume: Song 44 Orlando Gibbons

860.   Sleep! downy sleep! come close mine eyes
            18 octosyllables   Thomas Flatman
            2 decasyllables
        1674 Poems and Songs, pp. 48-49
            ℓ. 3: "Sweet slumbers come and chase away"
        1701 Divine Companion, with tune,
             p. 27   Jer. Clarke

861.   So cause us, Lord, to think upon
            C. M. D.   4 sts.   George Wither
        1623 Hymns and Songs, No. LXXXVII
        Tune in same volume: Song 3 Orlando Gibbons

862.   So foolish, so absurd am I
            C. M. D.   5 sts.   [John Mason]
            C. M.   1 st.
        1693 Penetential Cries, No. IV, p. 8
        No tune given but intended to be sung

863.   So much who knows, that he can say
            10 octosyllables   5 sts.   George Wither
        1641 Hal. Pt. 2, No. 1, pp. 227-228
        Suggested tune: The Lamentation

864.   So oft as neighbours disagree
             C. M. D.   5 sts.   George Wither
         1641 <u>Hal</u>. Pt. 3, No. XXXII, pp. 416-417
         Suggested tune: <u>Psalm 23</u>

865.   So powerful are the faithful cries
             C. M. D.   3 sts.   George Wither
         1641 <u>Hal</u>. Pt. 1, No. LXIIII, pp. 121-122
         Suggested tune: <u>Psalm 23</u>

866.   So sharp and bitter be the wrongs
             C. M. D.   3 sts.   George Wither
         1641 <u>Hal</u>. Pt. 1, No. XCIX, pp. 193-195
         Suggested tune: <u>Psalm 4</u>

867.   Some, have a custom, when they bring
             C. M. D.   6 sts.   George Wither
         1641 Hal. Pt. 1, No. XLI, pp. 66-68
         Suggested tune: <u>Psalm 4</u>

868.   Some think there is no earthly state
             C. M. D.   10 sts.   George Wither
         1641 <u>Hal</u>. Pt. 3, No. LII, pp. 459-462
         Suggested tune: <u>Psalm 15</u>

869.   Sometime, Oh Lord! at least in show
             L. M. D.   6 sts.   George Wither
         1641 <u>Hal</u>. Pt. 1, No. LXXXII, pp. 155-157
         Suggested tune: <u>10 Com.</u>

870.   Sorrow betide my sins! must smart so soon
             10.10. 6. 6.10.10   8 sts. [Christopher Harvey]
         1641 <u>The Synagogue</u>, pp. 24-26
             ℓ . <u>2</u>: "Seize on my Saviours tender flesh,
                scarce grown"
         1754 <u>C. H. C. G.</u>, Pt. I, No. 379, pp. 220-221
             10.<u>10</u>   13 sts.
             Begins: "Seize on my Saviours tender flesh,
                scarce grown"
             Tune to be selected by meter from appended
             <u>Table of Metres and Tunes</u>

871.   Strange truth, that the selfsame should be
             See: Mysterious truth! that   Jeremy Taylor
                the selfsame should be

872.   Stupendous love! That I so soon should be

irreg.   6 sts.   Lancelot Addison
1699 Devotional Poems, pp. 60-62
1754 C.H.C.G., Pt. I, No. 503, p. 293
10.10.10.10.10.10   5 sts.
Tune to be selected by meter from appended
Table of Metres and Tunes

873.   **Sure, you may be that orient light
       **8.7.8.7.8.7.8.7.8.7 (6 sts.) [Faithfull Teate]
       1754 C.H.C.G., Pt. I, No. 388, pp. 225-226
       Tune to be selected by meter from appended
       Table of Metres and Tunes

874.   Surpassing Lord, whose mercies have surpast
       8.8.8.8.8.8   John Quarles
       1663 Divine Meditations...With...Divine Ejacula-
       tions, p. 154

875.   Surrounding hosts of enemies
       C.M.D.   4 sts.   Thomas Shepherd
       1743 Spiritual Songs, No. XVII
       No tune given but intended to be sung

876.   Sweet day, so cool, so calm, so bright
       8.8.8.4   4 sts.   George Herbert
       1633 The Temple, p. 80
       1852 Hys. for Christian Ch. and Hm., 9th ed.,
       No. 515
       Choice of tunes from other books

877.   Sweet Infancy!
       4.8.4.4.8   4 sts.   Thomas Traherne
       1903 Poems and Centuries of Meditations,
       pp. 23-24
       1931 Songs of Praise, with tune,
       No. 651   Jane Joseph

878.   Sweet Jesu, why, why dost thou love
       C.M.   10 sts.; Amen   John Austin
       1672 (1st ed. 1668) Devotions, No. XXX,
       pp. 269-270
       1701 Devot. ed. H., p. 360; tune p. 1, separate
       section

879.   Sweet Jesus is the name
       See: Let others take their   John Austin
       course

880.   **Sweet Jesus with thy mother mild
          **8. 8. 8. 8   10 ℓ ℓ .   William Blundell
          1946 Alfred Noyes, ed., The   of Crosby
              Golden Book of Catholic Poetry, p. 66

881.   Sweet place, sweet place alone
          6. 6. 6. 6   6 sts.   Samuel Crossman
          8. 8   Refrain
          1678 The Young Man's Divine Meditations,
              pp. 423-425
          *A Sel. of Ps. and Hys: Kemble, with tune,
              No. 598
          Pt. II of "Sweet place, sweet place alone" be-
              gins: "Jerusalem on high"
          *1780 Wesleyan Hymn Book, with tune, No. 942
          *cento from the two parts: "Earth's but a
              sorry tent"

882.   **Sweet Saviour! from whose fivefold bleeding wound
          **14 decasyllables   Barnaby Barnes
          **1595 A Divine Centurie of Spirituall Sonnets
          1815 Reprint, p. 2

883.   Sweet slumbers come and chase away
          See: Sleep! downey sleep!   Thomas Flatman

884.   Sweet were the days, when thou didst lodge with lot
          10. 10. 10. 10. 8   4 sts.   George Herbert
          1633 The Temple, pp. 91-92
          1754 C. H. C. G., Pt. I, No. 363, p. 215
          10. 10. 10. 10   4 sts.
          Tune to be selected by meter from appended
              Table of Metres and Tunes

885.   Sweetest Saviour, if my soul
          7. 6. 7. 6. 7. 7. 7. 7   4 sts.   George Herbert
          1633 The Temple, p. 107
          *1739 Hymnes & Sacred Poems, with
              tune   J. Wesley
          *Begins: "Saviour, if thy precious love"

886.   Take heed my heart, for in my breast
          L. M. D.   7 sts.   George Wither
          1641 Hal. Pt. 3, No. XVIII, pp. 384-386
          Suggested tune: Psalm 51

887.   Take heed, my heart, how thou let in

C. M. D.   8 sts.   George Wither
1641 Hal. Pt. 1, No. XCVI, pp. 187-190
Suggested tune: The Te Deum

888.   Teach me, my God and King
        S. M.   6 sts.   George Herbert
        1633 The Temple, pp. 178-179
        *1738 Collection of Psalms, and Hymns, J. Wesley
        altered version
        1754 C. H. C. G., Pt. I, No. 365, p. 215
        S. M.   4 sts.
        Tune to be selected by meter from appended
        Table of Metres and Tunes

889.   Teach us by his example, Lord
        L. M. D.   3 sts.   George Wither
        1623 Hymns and Songs, No. LXIV
        Tune in same volume: Song 44 Orlando Gibbons

890.   **Tears have done
        **3.4.6.6.8.8.10.10.8.8.6.6.4.3   Joseph Beaumont
        10.10
        **c.1643 Minor Poems, MS.
        **Marked: To a Base and 2 Trebles
        1914 Reprint, p. 154

891.   Tell me you bright stars that shine
        7.7.7.7   10 sts.; Amen   John Austin
        1672 (1st ed. 1668) Devotions, No. XXXVIII,
        pp. 348-349
        1701 Devot. ed. H., p. 476; tune p. 11, separate
        section

892.   That doleful night when our dear Lord
        L. M.   8 sts.   Joseph Stennett
        1697 Hys. in Commem., No. III, p. 3
        Suggested tune: Psalm 100

893.   That heart is harder than a stone
        C. M. D.   4 sts.   [Thomas Shepherd]
        1693 Penetential Cries, No. XXV, p. 39
        No tune given but intended to be sung

894.   That rage, (as David's sore declared)
        L. M. D.   3 sts.   George Wither
        1641 Hal. Pt. 2, No. XLV, pp. 315-316
        Suggested tune: The 10 Com.

895.   That rage whereof the Psalm doth say
             L. M. D.   3 sts.   George Wither
         1623 Hymns and Songs, No. LXV, p. 48
             Tune in same volume: Song 44   Orlando Gibbons

896.   That so thy blessed birth, Oh Christ
             8. 8. 8. 8. 8. 8   4 sts.   George Wither
         1623 Hymns and Songs, No. XLIX, p. 40
             Tune in same volume: Song 9   Orlando Gibbons

897.   **The badge of faith bids, ne'er forget
             **L. M.   6 sts.   [Richard Crashaw]
         1754 C. H. C. G., Pt. I, No. 400, pp. 230-231
             Tune to be selected by meter from appended
             Table of Metres and Tunes

898.   **The birds that here so merrily do sing
             **10. 10. 10. 10. 10. 10   3 sts.   Unknown
         1927 The Evolution of the English Hymn,
             Frederick Gillman, p. 159

899.   The blessed Virgin travail'd without pain
             irreg.   21 ℓ ℓ .; Amen   Jeremy Taylor
         1655 Festival Hymnes appended to The Golden
             Grove, p. 150
         ℓ . 2: "And lodged in an Inne"
         1754 C. H. C. G., Pt. I, No. 405, p. 232
             4. 4. 4. 6. 6. 2. 4. 4. 4. 6   2 sts.
             Begins: "Lodg'd in an inn"
             Tune to be selected by meter from appended
             Table of Metres and Tunes

900.   **The constant Christian still doth good pursue
             10. 10   8 sts.   George Herbert
         1754 C. H. C. G., Pt. I, No. 272, p. 218
             Tune to be selected by meter from appended
             Table of Metres and Tunes

901.   The day is now return'd
             6. 8. 6. 8. 4. 4. 6. 4. 4. 6   8 sts.   George Wither
         1641 Hal. Pt. 2, No. XVIII, pp. 262-265
             Suggested tune: In sad and ashie weeds

902.   The favour, Lord, which of thy grace
             C. M. D.   25 sts.   George Wither

1623 Hymns and Songs, No. LXXXIII
Tune in same volume: Song 3 Orlando Gibbons

903. The faithful shepherd from on high
L. M. D.   10 sts.   Henry More
1668 Divine Hymns appended to Divine Dialogues,
pp. 497-500

904. The fields, for prayer, Isa'ck chose
C. M. D.   5 sts.   George Wither
1641 Hal. Pt. 1, No. XXXI, pp. 51-52
Suggested tune: Psalm 4

905. The first which brought the blessed news
8. 8. 8. 8. 8. 8   7 sts.   George Wither
1641 Hal. Pt. 2, No. XXIX, pp. 283-285
Suggested tune: The Lords Prayer

906. The flow'rs which wash'd away almost
C. M. D.   2 sts.   George Wither
1641 Hal. Pt. 1, No. LXII, p. 117
Suggested tune: Psalm 4

907. The forty days are ending: And you go
irreg.   7 sts.   Lancelot Addison
1699 Devotional Poems, pp. 13-14
1754 C. H. C. G., Pt. I, No. 494, pp. 289-290
10. 10   16 sts.
Tune to be selected by meter from appended
Table of Metres and Tunes

908. **The God of bliss
**4. 4. 6. 4. 4. 6   6 sts.   John Norden
1845 Farr Vol. 2, p. 461

909. The holy son of God most high
L. M.   10 sts.   Henry More
1668 Divine Hymns appended to Divine Dialogues,
pp. 495-496
1931 Songs of Praise, with tune, No. 80
Melody from V. Schumann's Gesangbuch

910. The Lamb is eaten, and is yet again
irreg.   36 ℓ ℓ.; Amen Jeremy Taylor
1655 Festival Hymnes appended to The Golden
Grove, pp. 161-162
ℓ . 3: "The cup is full and mixt, and must be
drunk"

1754 C. H. C. G. , Pt. I, no. 407, p. 232
L. M.   4 sts.
Begins: "It must be drunk, the cup is mix'd"
Tune to be selected by meter from appended
Table of Metres and Tunes

911.   The Lord be thanked for his gifts
         C. M. D.   124 ℓℓ .   Unknown
       c.1559 The First Parte of the Booke of Psalmes,
            unpaged
         Tune in same volume   Unknown

912.   The Lord both heav'n and earth hath made
         C. M. D.   6 sts.   Henry More
       1668 Divine Hymns appended to Divine Dialogues,
            pp. 509-511

913.   The Lord of Sabbath let us praise
         C. M.   4 sts.   Seventeenth Century
       1754 C. H. C. G. , Pt. I, No. 493, p. 289
         Tune to be selected by meter from appended
         Table of Metres and Tunes

914.   The love of Christ, poor I! may touch upon
         10.10.10.10   11 sts.   John Bunyan
       1686 A Book for Boys and Girls, pp. 58-59

915.   The night is come like to the day
         irreg.   30 ℓℓ .   Sir Thomas Browne
       1642 Religio Medici, Pt. II, pp. 81-82
         From this: "The sun is gone: like to the day"
       1688 Harmonia Sacra, Vol. 2,
            with tune, pp. 23-24

916.   **The pleasant years that seem so swift that run
         **10.10.10.10.10.10   4 sts.   Anonymous
       1890 Palgrave, p. 2

917.   The prince of darkness, flush'd with victory
         34 decasyllables   Sir Matthew Hale
       1676 Contemplations, "Poems upon Christmas
            Day," No. II, pp. 504-505
       1754 C. H. C. G. , Pt. I, No. 412, pp. 234-235
         10.10   4 sts.
         Tune to be selected by meter from appended
         Table of Metres and Tunes

918.   The propagation of our kind
            C. M. D.   7 sts.   George Wither
            1641 Hal. Pt. 3, No. XII, pp. 372-374
            Suggested tune: Psalm 1

919.   The sev'ral Sundays of man's life
            See: O day most calm,   George Herbert
                most bright

920.   The sixth day's light may weekly bring
            10 octosyllables 5 sts.   George Wither
            1641 Hal. Pt. 2, No. VII, pp. 237-238
            Suggested tune: The Lamentation

921.   The spouse sought her beloved one
            C. M. D.   4 sts.   [Thomas Shepherd]
            1693 Penetential Cries, No. XXVIII, p. 42
            No tune given but intended to be sung

922.   The sun, hath since we last were here
            C. M. D.   5 sts.   George Wither
            1641 Hal. Pt. 2, No. XVI, pp. 259-260
            Suggested tune: Psalm 23

923.   The sun is gone, like to the day
            See: The night is come   Sir Thomas Browne

924.   **The sun of our soul's light! Thee would I call
            **14 decasyllables   Barnaby Barnes
            **1595 A Divine Centurie of Spirituall Sonnets
            1815 Reprint, p. 37

925.   The talents we possess
            6. 8. 6. 8. 4. 4. 6. 4. 4. 6   4 sts.   George Wither
            1641 Hal. Pt. 1, No. CIII, pp. 205-206
            Suggested tune: In sad and ashie weeds

926.   *The winds of God have changed their note
            14 ℓ ℓ .   Henry Vaughan
            *1678 Thalia Rediviva
            *1855 Hymns for the Church of England

927.   The world can neither give nor take
            See: My God, my reconciled   John Mason
                God

928.   **The world's bright comforter, whose beamsome light

         **14 decasyllables   Barnaby Barnes
     **1595 A Divine Centurie of Spirituall Sonnets
      1815 Reprint, p. 45

929.   The world will talk; and let the world talk on
           irreg.   2 sts.   Lancelot Addison
      1699 Devotional Poems, pp. 41-42

930.   There is a balsam, or indeed a blood
           See: Come bring thy gifts,   George Herbert
           if blessings were as slow

931.   There is a stream which issues forth
           See: My soul doth magnify the   John Mason
           Lord

932.   They are all gone into the world of light
           10. 8. 10. 8   10 sts.   Henry Vaughan
      1655 Silex Scintillans, Pt. II, pp. 4-6
       *From this: "Dear,   James Martineau
         beauteous death! the jewel of the just"
    *1873 Hymns of Praise and Prayer
     1931 Songs of Praise,
       with tune, No. 294   Traditional Irish Melody

933.   They, no mean place of trust, receive
           L. M. D.   7 sts.   George Wither
      1641 Hal. Pt. 3, No. V, pp. 358-360
      Suggested tune: Psalm 4

934.   They, Oh thrice holy, three in one!
           See: Those, Oh thrice holy!   George Wither

935.   They who their Father had forsook
           L. M. D.   5 sts.   George Wither
      1641 Hal. Pt. 2, No. LIII, pp. 326-327
      Suggested tune: The 10 Com.

936.   This day thy flesh, Oh Christ, did bleed
           L. M. D.   3 sts.   George Wither
      1623 Hys. and Songs, No. XLVIII, p. 39
      Tune in same volume: Song 44   Orlando Gibbons

937.   This day, the planets in the spheres
           L. M. D.   3 sts.   George Wither
      1641 Hal. Pt. 2, No. V, pp. 234-235
      Suggested tune: Psalm 100

938.   This day we sing
               irreg. (24 ℓ ℓ .; Allelujah; Amen) Jeremy Taylor
          1655 Festival Hymnes appended to The Golden
               Grove, p. 151

939.   This empty world has now too long
               C. M. D.   5 sts.   [Thomas Shepherd]
          1693 Penetential Cries, No. IX, p. 16
          No tune given but intended to be sung

940.   This homely bush doth to mine eyes expose
               10.10.10.10   26 ℓ ℓ .   John Bunyan
          1686 A Book for Boys and Girls, pp. 44-45
          Tune in same volume

941.   This is the day the Lord hath made (not Psalm 118)
               L. M. D.   5 sts.   George Wither
          1623 Hymns and Songs, No. LVI, p. 43
          Tune in same volume: Song 44 Orlando Gibbons

942.   This is the gift, thy gift, O Lord
               L. M.   7 sts.   Samuel Crossman
          1678 The Young-Man's Divine Meditations,
               pp. 413-414
          [1931] The Hymn Book of the Modern Church,
               p. 98

943.   This is the month, and this the happy morn
               10.10.10.10.10.10.12   4 sts.   John Milton
          1629 Introduction to Ode On the morning of
               Christ's nativity
          1673 Poems, p. 1
               st. 13, ℓ . 1: "Ring out, ye crystal spheres"
          1872 Hymns for the Use of the University of Ox-
               ford in St. Mary's Church, No. IX
          Tune not given but intended to be sung

944.   This morning brings to mind O God!
               L. M. D.   3 sts.   George Wither
          1641 Hal. Pt. 2, No. III, pp. 231-232
          Suggested tune: Psalm 100

945.   Those, oh, thrice holy three in one
               8. 8. 8. 8. 8. 8   10 sts.   George Wither
          1623 Hymns and Songs, No. LIX, p. 45
          Tune in same volume: Song 9 Orlando Gibbons

946.   Thou art all love, my dearest Lord
        C. M.   6 sts.   Joseph Stennett
        1697 Hys. in Commem., No. II, p. 2
        No tune given but intended to be sung

947.   Thou art my life; if thou but turn away
        See: Why dost thou shade   Francis Quarles
        thy lovely face? O why

948.   **Thou art the way to thee alone
        **C. M.   4 sts.   John Donne
        1870 The Hymnal Companion to Book of Common
        Prayer, No. 228
        Suggested tune: Any C. M. tune

949.   Thou dost from every season, Lord
        8. 8. 8. 8. 8. 8   6 sts.   George Wither
        1623 Hymns and Songs, No. LXXXIV, p. 59
        Tune in same volume: Song 9 Orlando Gibbons

950.   **Thou God for ever blest
        **irreg.   3 sts.   H. W.
        1696 Nahum Tate, Miscellanae Sacra, pp. 58-59

951.   Thou, God, that rul'st and reignst in light
        C. M. D.   9 sts.   William Hunnis
        1597 The Poore Widowes Mite, bound with Seven
        Sobs of a Sorrowfull Soule for Sinne, pp. 33-
        34
        Tune in same volume   William Hunnis

952.   Thou gracious hearer of requests
        8. 8. 8. 8. 8. 8   John Quarles
        1663 Divine Meditations... With... Divine Ejacula-
        tions, p. 148

953.   Thou Great God, now and ever blessed
        8. 8. 8. 8. 8. 8   20 sts.   Thomas Heywood
        1635 The Hierarchie of the Blessed Angells,
        pp. 401-404

954.   Thou hast made me: and shall thy work decay
        See: As due by many titles I re- John Donne
        sign   (altered)

955.   **Thou, Lord, my mortal eyes unseen
        **L. M.   6 sts.   John Mason
        1808 Trinity Church, pp. 131-132   (altered)

Suggested tunes: Sharp or Flat tune

956.   Thou Lord my power and wisdom art
          See: But that thou art my   George Herbert
                wisdome Lord   (altered)

957.   Thou Lord, who daily feed'st thy sheep
          See: My Lord my Love was   John Mason
                crucified

958.   Thou Lord, who raised'st heaven and earth
          C. M. D.   4 sts.   John Mason
          C. M.   1 st.
          1683 Spiritual Songs, No. IV, pp. 12-14
          st. 3, ℓ. 1: "In thee I live and move and am"
          No tune given but intended to be sung

959.   Thou righteous hearer of requests
          8. 8. 8. 8. 8. 8   John Quarles
          1663 Divine Meditations... With... Divine Ejacula-
                tions, p. 129

960.   Thou spread'st a weekly table, Lord
          L. M.   7 sts.   [Thomas Shepherd]
          1693 Penetential Cries, No. XXX, p. 45
          Suggested tune: Psalm 100

961.   Thou that hast given so much to me
          8. 8. 8. 2   8 sts.   George Herbert
          1633 The Temple, pp. 116-117

962.   **Thou the dear sinners friend, to thee
          **L. M.   7 sts.   George Herbert
          1754 C. H. C. G. , Pt. I, No. 369, pp. 216-217
          Tune to be selected by meter from appended
          Table of Metres and Tunes

963.   Thou wast, O God: and thou wast blest
          C. M. D.   6 sts.   John Mason
          1683 Spiritual Songs, No. III, pp. 9-12
          No tune given but intended to be sung

964.   Tho' I am fallen from my God
          C. M. D.   4 sts.   [Thomas Shepherd]
          1693 Penetential Cries, No. XVIII, p. 29
          No tune given but intended to be sung

965.   Though in my limbs I crippl'd am
         8. 8. 8. 8. 8. 8   6 sts.   George Wither
         1641 Hal. Pt. 3, No. XLVIII, pp. 451-452
         Suggested tune: The Lords Prayer

966.   Though knowledge must be got with pain
         L. M. D.   4 sts.   George Wither
         1641 Hal. Pt. 3, No. XLIIII, pp. 442-444
         Suggested tune: The 10 Com.

967.   Though princes courts defamed are
         C. M. D.   6 sts.   George Wither
         1641 Hal. Pt. 3, No. VII, pp. 362-364
         Suggested tunes: The Te Deum or Psalm 23

968.   Though thousands here, ten thousands there
         8. 8. 8. 8. 8. 8   John Quarles
         1663 Divine Meditations... With... Divine Ejacula-
              tions, p. 155

969.   Though, we have got an evil-name
         L. M. D.   7 sts.   George Wither
         1641 Hal. Pt. 3, LVI, pp. 469-471
         Suggested tune: The 10 Com.

970.   Thousands of thousands stand around
         See: How shall I sing the   John Mason
              Majesty

971.   Throw away thy rod
         5. 5. 3. 5   8 sts.   George Herbert
         1633 The Temple, pp. 173-174
         1737 Collection of Psalms and Hymns
         6. 6. 8. 6   8 sts.
         Begins: "O throw away thy rod"
         No tune given but intended to be sung

972.   Thy blessing, Lord, doth multiply
         C. M. D.   5 sts.   John Mason
         1683 Spiritual Songs, No. VIII, pp. 19-21
         No tune given but intended to be sung

973.   Thy gifts and graces manifold
         L. M. D.   3 sts.   George Wither
         1623 Hymns and Songs, No. LXX, p. 50
         Tune in same volume: Song 44
                                             Orlando Gibbons

974.   Thy gifts most, holy-spirit, be
         C. M. D.   6 sts.   George Wither
         1641 Hal. Pt. 3, No. XLII, pp. 438-440
         No tune given but intended to be sung

975.   **Thy heavenly kingdom here below
             **8. 8. 8. 8. 10. 10   3 sts.   Joseph Beaumont
         **c.1643 Minor Poems, MS.
             **Marked: To a Base and 2 Trebles
         1914 Reprint, p. 196

976.   Thy restless feet now cannot go
             See: Jesu no more it is   Richard Crashaw
                 full tide

977.   **Thy Saviour press'd to death, there ran
             **C. M.   3 sts.   [Sixteenth Century]
         1754 C. H. C. G., Pt. I, No. 428, p. 249
         Tune to be selected by meter from appended
         Table of Metres and Tunes

978.   Thy wondrous fasting to record
         L. M. D.   4 sts.   George Wither
         1623 Hymns and Songs, No. LI, p. 41
         Tune in same volume: Song 44
                                         Orlando Gibbons

979.   'Tis not for us, and our proud hearts
             8. 8. 6. 8. 8. 6   6 sts.; Amen   John Austin
         1672 (1st ed. 1668) Devotions, No. XXIV,
                 pp. 212-213
         1701 Devot. ed. H., p. 281; tune, p. 4, separate
         section

980.   **'Tis true indeed, that for a while
             **C. M.   29 sts.   [Sixteenth Century]
         1754 C. H. C. G., Pt. I, No. 425, pp. 246-248
         Tune to be selected by meter from appended
         Table of Metres and Tunes

981.   To bid each other now adieu
         C. M. D.   4 sts.   George Wither
         1641 Hal. Pt. 1, No. XXXIX, pp. 63-64
         Suggested tune: Psalm 133

982.   To blaze the rising of this glorious sun
             10. 10. 10. 10. 10. 10   4 sts.   Robert Southwell
         1634 Maeoniae, pp. 113-114

983.   To day the Lord of hosts invites
            C. M.   13 sts.   [Thomas Shepherd]
        1693 Penetential Cries, No. XXII, p. 34
        No tune given but intended to be sung

984.   To God, with heart and cheerful voice
            C. M. D.   5 sts.   George Wither
        1623 Hymns and Songs, No. LVII, p. 44
        Tune in same volume: Song 3
                                            Orlando Gibbons

985.   To grace (O Lord) a marriage-feast
            C. M. D.   4 sts.   George Wither
        1641 Hal. Pt. 1, No. XLV, pp. 74-75
        Suggested tune: The Te Deum

986.   To praise, Oh God, and honour thee
            L. M. D.   4 sts.   George Wither
        1623 Hymns and Songs, No. LXXVI, p. 52
        Tune in same volume: Song 44
                                            Orlando Gibbons

987.   To praise redeeming love
            6. 6. 6. 6. 4. 4. 4. 4   6 sts.   [Thomas Shepherd]
        1693 Penetential Cries, No. XIII, p. 22
        Suggested tune: Psalm 148

988.   To rip up God's great counsels who shall strive
            10.10.10.10.10.10.10.12 (15 sts.) Thomas Heywood
        1635 The Hierarchie of the Blessed Angells,
             pp. 558-561

989.   To that sweet Lamb, which did sustain
            8. 8. 8. 8. 8. 8   John Quarles
        1663 Divine Meditations... With... Divine Ejacula-
             tions, p. 149

990.   To thee, the saints that in thee trust
            8. 8. 4. 4. 10   23 sts.   Thomas Heywood
        1635 The Hierarchie of the Blessed Angells,
             pp. 266-269

991.   To those that in folly
            6.5.6.5.6.5.6.5.6.5.6.5   17 sts.   George Wither
        1641 Hal. Pt. 1, No. LXXXVII, pp. 163-170
        No tune given but intended to be sung

992.   To us our God commends his love
         C. M.   7 sts.   Joseph Stennett
         1697 Hys. in Commem., No. V, p. 5
         No tune given but intended to be sung

993.   To you, dear Father, my complaints I'll bring
             irreg.   5 sts.   Lancelot Addison
         1699 Devotional Poems, pp. 62-64

994.   To thy apostles thou hast taught
         C. M. D.   4 sts.   George Wither
         1623 Hymns and Songs, No. LXIX, p. 49
         Tune in same volume: Song 3
                                              Orlando Gibbons

995.   To yield us profit with delights
         C. M. D.   4 sts.   George Wither
         1641 Hal. Pt. 1, No. XXX, pp. 49-50
         Suggested tune: Psalm 4

996.   Tongues of fire from heaven descend
             irreg.   18 ℓℓ.; Amen   Jeremy Taylor
         1655 Festival Hymnes appended to The Golden
             Grove, pp. 165-166
         ℓ. 12: "Lord let the flames of holy charity"

997.   **Triumphant conqueror of death and hell
             **14 decasyllables   Barnaby Barnes
         **1595 A Divine Centurie of Spirituall Sonnets
             1815 Reprint, p. 37

998.   True God, true life, from, by, in whom all things
             70 decasyllables   Thomas Heywood
         1635 The Hierarchie of the Blessed Angells,
             pp. 189-190

999.   Tune now yourselves, my heart strings high
         L. M.   8 sts.; Amen   John Austin
         1672 (1st ed. 1668) Devotions, No. XXII, pp. 194-
             195
         1701 Devot. ed. H., p. 254; tune p. 2, separate
             section

1000.   **Tune we our heart strings high
             **6. 6. 6. 6. 8. 8   Joseph Beaumont
         **c.1643 Minor Poems, MS.
             **Marked: To a Base and 2 Trebles
         1914 Reprint, p. 197

1001.   Turn in, my Lord, turn in to me
          8. 6. 8. 6. 8. 8   3 sts.   Christopher Harvey
          6. 6. 11. 11
          1640 The Synagogue, p. 8

1002. **Turn not away the sunshine of thy face
          **14 decasyllables   Barnaby Barnes
          **1595 A Divine Centurie of Spirituall Sonnets
          1815 Reprint, p. 31

1003.   Types of eternal rest, fair buds of bliss
          See: Bright shadows of true   Henry Vaughan
          rest! some shoots of bliss

1004.   *Unction the Christian name implies
          *1721 Hymns for all the Festivals   Thomas Ken
          of the Year

1005.   Unfold thy face, unmask the ray
          26 octosyllables   [Christopher Harvey]
          1640 The Synagogue, p. 10-11

1006. **Unhappy soul, that thou should'st force
          **C. M.   5 sts.   Seventeenth Century
          1754 C. H. C. G., Pt. I, No. 508, p. 295
          Tune to be selected by meter from appended
          Table of Metres and Tunes

1007.   Unless, Oh Lord, thy grace thy lend
          C. M. D.   6 sts.   George Wither
          1641 Hal. Pt. 3, No. XXXV, pp. 421-423
          Suggested tunes: Psalm 4 or 5 or 6

1008. **Unto my spirit lend an angel's wing
          **14 decasyllables   Barnaby Barnes
          **1595 A Divine Centurie of Spirituall Sonnets
          1815 Reprint, p. 36

1009.   Unworthy, though, O Lord, we are
          C. M. D.   5 sts.   George Wither
          1641 Hal. Pt. 1, No. XLII, pp. 68-70
          Suggested tune: Psalm 23

1010. **View me, Lord, a work of thine
          **7. 7. 7. 7   5 sts.   Thomas Campion
          **1613 Two Bookes of Ayres, Bk. I, No. 5
          **Tune in same volume   Thomas Campion
          1909 Campion's Works, p. 119

1011.   Wake all my hopes, lift up your eyes
             C. M.   11 sts.; Amen   John Austin
          1672 (1st ed. 1668) Devotions, No. XXXVII,
             pp. 338-339
          1701 Devot. ed. H., p. 463; tune p. 1, separate
             section

1012.   *Wake, and lift up thyself, my heart
             See: Awake my soul, and   Thomas Ken
             with the sun

1013.   Wake my soul, rise from this bed
             7. 6. 7. 6   8 sts.; Amen   John Austin
          1672 (1st ed. 1668) Devotions, No. II, pp. 20-21
          1701 Devot. ed. H., p. 27; tune, p. 6, separate
             section

1014.   Wake now, my soul, and humbly hear
             C. M.   8 sts.; Amen   John Austin
          1672 (1st ed. 1668) Devotions, No. V, pp. 49-50
          1701 Devot. ed. H., p. 56; tune p. 1, separate
             section

1015.   Wake, O my soul; awake, and raise
             8.8.8.8.8.8.4.4.4.4   4 sts.   Phineas Fletcher
          1633 Poeticall Miscellanies, appended to the
             Purple Isle, pp. 95-96

1016.   We do acknowledge thee, Oh Lord
             C. M. D.   6 sts.   George Wither
          1641 Hal. Pt. 2, No. XXXVIII, pp. 302-304
          Suggested tune: Psalm 117

1017.   We love thee, Lord, we praise thy name
             L. M. D.   4 sts.   George Wither
          1623 Hymns and Songs, No. LXXXVIII, p. 61
          Tune in same volume: Song 44
                                               Orlando Gibbons

1018.   We praise O God! we honor thee
             C. M. D.   3 sts.   George Wither
          1641 Hal. Pt. 1, No. XXXV, pp. 57-58
          Suggested tune: The Magnificat

1019.   We sing to Him whose wisdom form'd the ear
             10.10.10.10.10.10   3 sts.   Nathaniel Ingelo
             10.10   Chorus

      1660 Bentivolio and Urania, Bk. IV, p. 150
      1677 The Whole Book of Psalms, with tune p. 293
                                          John Playford

1020.   We sing to Thee whose wisdom
          See: We sing to Him whose   Nathaniel Ingelo
          wisdom

1021.   We that have passed in slumber sweet
          See: You that have spent   George Gascoigne
          the silent night

1022.   We, whom affairs employed keep
          8.6.8.6.4.4.6.4.4.6   8 sts.   George Wither
          1641 Hal. Pt. 3, No. XXXVII, pp. 427-430
          No tune given but intended to be sung

1023.   Welcome sweet and sacred cheer
          7.3.7.7.3.7   9 sts.   George Herbert
          1633 The Temple, pp. 175-177
          st. 1, ℓ. 3: "With me, in me live and dwell"
          1754 C.H.C.G., Pt. I, No. 378, p. 220
          7.7.3.7.3.8.8.7   5 sts.
          Begins: "With me, in me, live and dwell"
          Tune to be selected by meter from appended
          Table of Metres and Tunes

1024.   Welcome, white day! a thousand suns
          L.M.   16 sts.   Henry Vaughan
          1654 Silex Scintillans, Pt. II, pp. 6-8

1025.   We'll praise our risen Lord
          See: Immortal praise be   Joseph Stennett
          given

1026. **What a blessed change I find
          **7.7.7.7.7.7   [Sixteenth Century]
          1754 C.H.C.G., Pt. I, No. 430, pp. 249-250
          Tune to be selected by meter from appended
          Table of Metres and Tunes

1027.   What a celestial virtue's chastity
          irreg.   3 sts.   Lancelot Addison
          1699 Devotional Poems, pp. 65-66
          1754 C.H.C.G., Pt. I, No. 520, p. 299
          Tune to be selected by meter from appended
          Table of Metres and Tunes

1028. **What a gracious God have we
         **7. 7. 7. 7   5 sts.   William Austin
      [1931] The Hymn Book of the Modern Church,
             p. 91

1029.   What are the heav'ns, O God of heaven
         C. M. D.   4 sts.   John Mason
         C. M.   1 st.
         1683 Spiritual Songs, No. XXVI, pp. 56-58
         No tune given but intended to be sung

1030.   What ails my heart, that in my breast
         C. M. D.   4 sts.   George Wither
         1641 Hal. Pt. 1, No. XX, pp. 29-30
         Suggested tunes: Psalms 33 or 34

1031.   What glorious light
         irreg. 21 ℓ ℓ.; Allelujah; Amen   Jeremy Taylor
         1655 Festival Hymnes appended to The Golden
              Grove, p. 164

1032.   What have I in this barren land
         See: I sojourn in a vale of tears   John Mason

1033.   What hellish doubt! what cursed fear
         C. M. D.   7 sts.   George Wither
         1641 Hal. Pt. 1, No. XCI, pp. 175-177
         Suggested tune: The Te Deum

1034. **What helps it those
         **4.6.4.6.4.6.4.6.4.6.4.6   4 sts. William Austin
         1940 Lord David Cecil, ed., The Oxford Book of
              Christian Verse, pp. 116-119

1035.   What helps it to kill me each day
         See: Kill me not ev'ry day   George Herbert

1036.   What I possess, or what I crave
         8. 8. 8. 8. 8. 8   John Quarles
         1663 Divine Meditations... With... Divine Ejacula-
              tions, p. 167

1037.   What is there Lord
         4.6.4.6.4.6.4.6.4.6.4.6   7 sts.   George Wither
         1641 Hal. Pt. 1, No. LXXIX, pp. 147-150
         Suggested tune: A Hermit Poor

1038.   What is there Lord, what is in me
            8. 8. 8. 8. 8. 8   John Quarles
            1663 Divine Meditations... With... Divine Ejacula-
               tions, p. 172

1039.   What line can fathom, Lord
            6. 6. 6. 6. 4. 4. 4. 4   5 sts.   Thomas Shepherd
            1743 (16th ed.) Spiritual Songs, No. XV
            Suggested tune: Psalm 148

1040.   What mighty conqueror do we see
            L. M.   10 sts.   Joseph Stennett
            1697 Hys. in Commem., No. XXXVI, p. 47
            Suggested tune: Psalm 100

1041.   What needs a conscience, clear and bright
            See: If this worlds friends   Henry Vaughan
            might see but once

1042.   What plenties (O thrice gracious Lord!)
            C. M. D.   4 sts.   George Wither
            1641 Hal. Pt. 1, No. XXXII, pp. 52-54
            Suggested tune: Psalm 4

1043.   What shall I render to my God
            C. M. D.   7 sts.   John Mason
            C. M.   1 st.
            1683 Spiritual Songs, No. II, pp. 6-9
            No tune given but intended to be sung

1044.   What shall we do to thee, O God
            C. M.   8 sts.   John Norden
            1845 Farr, Vol. 2, p. 460

1045.   What spring and summer did produce
            8. 8. 8. 8. 8. 8   6 sts.   George Wither
            1641 Hal. Pt. 2, No. XXI, pp. 269-270
            Suggested tune: The Lords Prayer

1046.   What though the comforts of the light
            C. M. D.   4 sts.   George Wither
            1641 Hal. Pt. 1, No. XVI, pp. 23-24
            Suggested tunes: Psalms 19 or 20 or 21

1047.   What wondrous things do we behold
            C. M.   9 sts.   Joseph Stennett
            1697 Hys. in Commem., No. XXXIII, p. 43
            No tune given but intended to be sung

1048.   What words what voices can we bring
         C. M.   8 sts.
         1715 Divine Companion, 3rd ed., with tune,
             p. 16   Jer. Clarke

1049.   Whatever equity commands
         C. M. D.   5 sts.   George Wither
         1641 Hal. Pt. 3, No. LV, pp. 467-468
         Suggested tune: Psalm 15

1050.   Whatever others do intend to do
             irreg.   6 sts.   Lancelot Addison
         1699 Devotional Poems, pp. 4-6
         Also see: You that with just Zacheus do desire
         1754 C. H. C. G., Pt. I, No. 506, pp. 294-295
         Tune to be selected by meter from appended
         Table of Metres and Tunes

1051.   Whatever story of their cruelty
             10. 10. 10. 10. 10. 10   Richard Crashaw
         1648 Steps to the Temple, p. 9
         1754 C. H. C. G., Pt. I, No. 396, p. 229
         Begins: "What stories of their cruelty"
         Tune to be selected by meter from appended
         Table of Metres and Tunes

1052   **What's this morn bright eye to me
             **10 septisyllables   2 sts.   Joseph Beaumont
         **c.1643 Minor Poems, MS.
         1914 Reprint, p. 325

1053.   Whatsoe're my motives were
             7. 7. 7. 7. 7. 7. 7. 7   6 sts.   George Wither
         1641 Hal. Pt. 3, No. XXIX, pp. 410-412
         No tune given but intended to be sung

1054.   When Achan for his lawless-prize
         C. M. D.   7 sts.   George Wither
         1641 Hal. Pt. 3, No. LIX, pp. 475-477
         Suggested tune: We praise thee God

1055.   When Adam was deceived
         6. 6. 6. 6   29 sts.   John Bunyan
         1686 A Book for Boys and Girls, pp. 2-7

1056.   When all thy mercies, O my God
         C. M.   12 sts.   Seventeenth Century

1754 C. H. C. G. , Pt. I, No. 531, pp. 302-303
Tune to be selected by meter from appended
Table of Metres and Tunes

1057.   When blessed Marie wip'd her Saviour's feet
        10. 10. 10. 8. 8. 10   3 sts.   George Herbert
        1633 The Temple, p. 168
        1754 C. H. C. G. , Pt. I, No. 374, pp. 218-219
        Tune to be selected by meter from appended
        Table of Metres and Tunes

1058.   When Christ from death, to life did rise
        L. M. D.   4 sts.   George Wither
        1641 Hal. Pt. 2, No. XLII, pp. 311-312
        Suggested tune: The Lord's Prayer

1059.   When Christ his body up had borne
        1668 Divine Hymns appended   Henry More
            to Divine Dialogues, pp. 504-506
        1864 Church Pastorals, with tune,
            No. 248
        Begins: "On all the earth thy spirit shower"
        Also from above: "Father if justly"

1060.   When Christ unto Jerusalem
        See: When Jesus to Jerusalem   George Wither

1061.   When Christ our Lord incarnate was
        See: When Jesus Christ   George Wither
            incarnate was

1062.   When Christ was risen from the dead
        8. 8. 8. 8. 8. 8   4 sts.   George Wither
        1623 Hymns and Songs, No. LXII, p. 47
        Tune in same volume, Song 9
                                        Orlando Gibbons

1063.   When from mortality and things below
        irreg.   4 sts.   Lancelot Addison
        1699 Devotional Poems, pp. 36-38

1064.   When from your dying breath I hear from you
        irreg.   6 sts.   Lancelot Addison
        1699 Devotional Poems, pp. 58-60

1065.   When God at first made man
        6. 10. 10. 10. 6   4 sts.   George Herbert

1633 The Temple, pp. 153-154
*1899 Hymns for Use in the Chapel of Marlborough
College, with tune

1066.   When God the first foundations laid
         L. M.   13 sts.   Henry More
         1668 Divine Hymns appended to Divine Dialogues,
         pp. 507-509

1067.   When hearty thanks we render not
         C. M. D.   2 sts.   George Wither
         1641 Hal. Pt. 1, No. LXVII, pp. 125-126
         Suggested tune: The Te Deum

1068.   When I begin sadly to think upon
              62 decasyllables   Sir Matthew Hale
         1676 Contemplations "Poems upon Christmas Day"
              No. IV, pp. 506-508 (written 1652)
         1754 C. H. C. G., Pt. I, No. 413, pp. 235-236
         10.10   29 sts.
         Tune to be selected by meter from appended
         Table of Metres and Tunes

1069.   When I look back and in myself behold
         10. 10. 10. 10. 10. 10   6 sts.   Thomas Vaux
         1890 Palgrave, p. 2   (2nd Baron Vaux
                                             of Harrowden)

1070.   When is it fitter to begin
         C. M. D.   5 sts.   George Wither
         1641 Hal. Pt. 1, No. XXXIII, pp. 54-55
         Suggested tune: Psalm 4

1071.   When Jesus Christ incarnate was
         8. 8. 8. 8. 8. 8.   6 sts.   George Wither
         1623 Hymns and Songs, No. XLV, p. 37
         Tune in same volume: Song 9
                                             Orlando Gibbons

1072.   When Jesus to Jerusalem
         C. M. D.   4 sts.   George Wither
         1623 Hymns and Songs, No. LIII, p. 41
         Tune in same volume: Song 3
                                             Orlando Gibbons

1073.   When land and sea that mixed were
         C. M. D.   4 sts.   George Wither

1641 Hal. Pt. 2, No. IIII, pp. 232-234
Suggested tune: The Te Deum

1074.   When Lord, O when shall we
6.6.4.4.10.6.6.8.10.4.10.8.8.8.8.10 Jeremy Taylor
2 sts.; Amen
1655 Festival Hymnes appended to The Golden
Grove, pp. 145-146

1075.   When, Lord, shall Jew and Gentile raise
L. M.   5 sts.   Thomas Shepherd
1743 (16th ed.) Spiritual Songs, No. XXVI
Suggested tune: 100 Psalm

1076.   When Lord, we call to mind those things
C. M. D.   8 sts.   George Wither
1623 Hymns and Songs, No. XC, p. 61
Tune in same volume: Song 3
Orlando Gibbons

1077. **When love the king of bounty, did
**C. M.   7 sts.   Joseph Beaumont
**c.1643 Minor Poems, MS.
1914 Reprint, pp. 245-246

1078.   When Mary wip'd her Saviour's feet
See: When blessed Marie   George Herbert
wip'd her Saviour's feet

1079.   When one among the twelve there was
C. M. D.   3 sts.   George Wither
1623 Hymns and Songs, No. LXVII, p. 49
Tune in same volume: Song 67
[M. Frost lists tune as Beatus Vir in Prys 1621.]

1080.   When one loud blast shall rend the deep
See: When through the north   Henry Vaughan
a fire shall rush

1081.   When one of thine, did false become
C. M. D.   3 sts.   George Wither
1641 Hal. Pt. 2, No. XLVII, pp. 317-318
Suggested tune: Psalm 4

1082.   When quiet in my house I sit
8. 8. 8. 8. 8. 8   3 sts.   Charles Wesley
1839 Hendee, No. 572
No tune given but intended to be sung

1083.   When rising from the bed of death
         C. M.   6 sts.   Seventeenth Century
         1754 C. H. C. G., Pt. I, No. 505, p. 294
         Tune to be selected by meter from appended
         Table of Metres and Tunes

1084.   When Sampson's mother was foretold
         L. M. D.   4 sts.   George Wither
         1641 Hal. Pt. 3, No. XLIX, pp. 453-454
         No tune given but intended to be sung

1085.   *When shall this time of travail cease
         **C. M.   20 sts.   Thomas Bryce
         1845 Farr Vol. 1, p. 175

1086.   When sin had brought death, with a train
         L. M.   10 sts.   Joseph Stennett
         1697 Hys. in Commem., No. XIV, p. 16
         Suggested tune: Psalm 100

1087.   *When the angels all are singing
         **8. 8. 8. 8. 8. 8   7 sts.   Nicholas Breton
         1845 Farr Vol. 1, p. 194

1088.   When thou hast spent the lingering day
         8. 6. 8. 6   38 ℓℓ.   George Gascoigne
         1575 Posies in section called Flowers, pp. xxiiii-
              xxv
         1947 Hymn Book of the King's School, No. 30
         No tune given but intended to be sung

1089.   When thou would'st, Lord, afflict a land
         8. 8. 8. 8. 8. 8   4 sts.   George Wither
         1623 Hymns and Songs, No. LXXXIX, p. 61
         Tune in same volume: Song 9
                                        Orlando Gibbons

1090.   When through the north a fire shall rush
         C. M.   11 sts.   Henry Vaughan
         1650 Silex Scintillans, pp. 13-14
         st. 5, ℓ. 1: "When one loud blast shall rend
              the deep"

1091.   When virgin morn doth call thee
         See: When with the virgin   Robert Herrick
               morning

1092.   When we have all things of our own
            L. M. D.   4 sts.   George Wither
         1641 Hal. Pt. 1, No. LXXXVIII, pp. 170-172
         Suggested tune: Psalm 100

1093.   When wilt thou come unto me, Lord
            See: Alas, my God   [Thomas Shepherd]
               that we should be

1094.   When winds and seas do rage
            6. 7. 6. 7   3 sts.   Robert Herrick
         1647 Noble Numbers, p. 42

1095.   When winter fortunes cloud the brows
            8. 8. 8. 8. 8. 8   John Quarles
         1663 Divine Meditations... With... Divine Ejacula-
            tions, p. 172

1096.   When with the virgin morning thou do'st rise
            10. 10   Robert Herrick
         1931 Songs of Praise, with tune, No. 36   English
         Begins: "When virgin   Traditional Melody
            morn doth call thee"

1097.   When with your dying breath I hear from you
            irreg.   6 sts.   Lancelot Addison
         1699 Devotional Poems, pp. 58-60
         1754 C. H. C. G., Pt. I, No. 526, p. 300
            10. 10. 10. 10   4 sts.
         Tune to be selected by meter from appended
            Table of Metres and Tunes

1098.   When you a bitter enemy forgive
            irreg.   4 sts.   Lancelot Addison
         1699 Devotional Poems, pp. 78-79

1099.   Where God doth dwell, sure heaven is there
            See: My God, my reconciled   John Mason
               God

1100.   Where lies a sin, I'll drop a tear
            C. M. D.   4 sts.   [Thomas Shepherd]
         1693 Penetential Cries, No. XI, p. 19
         No tune given but intended to be sung

1101.   Where righteousness doth say
            6. 6. 6. 6. D.   8 sts.   Unknown

c.1559 The First parte of the Book of Psalms,
(unpaged)
Tune in same volume   Unknown

1102. Wherefore are the songs of praise
       11 septisyllables   5 sts.   George Wither
       1641 Hal. Pt. 2, No. XIII, pp. 252-254
       No tune given but intended to be sung

1103. Wherewith shall I a sinful worm
       L. M.   8 sts.   Joseph Stennett
       1697 Hys. in Commem., No. XVII, p. 20
       Suggested tune: Psalm 100

1104. **While Jesus on the lap of Mary lies
       **10.10   2 sts.   Richard Crashaw
       1754 C. H. C. G., Pt. I, No. 393, p. 229
       Tune to be selected by meter from appended
       Table of Metres and Tunes

1105. Whil'st Andrew, as a fisher fought
       L. M. D.   3 sts.   George Wither
       1641 Hal. Pt. 2, No. XLI, pp. 310-311
       Suggested tune: The 10 Com.

1106. Whilst others costly offerings bring
       C. M. D.   4 sts.   [Thomas Shepherd]
       1693 Penetential Cries, No. XII, p. 21
       No tune given but intended to be sung

1107. Whilst we endeavor to obey
       C. M. D.   5 sts.   George Wither
       1641 Hal. Pt. 1, No. LIIII, pp. 95-96
       Suggested tune: Psalm 4

1108. Whither, O whither art thou fled
       8. 4. 8. 4   14 sts.   George Herbert
       1633 The Temple, pp. 156-157
       st. 5 begins: "I sent a sigh to seek thee out"
       1737 Collection of Psalms and Hymns, No. XXXIX,
            p. 37
       Begins: "How swiftly wafted in a sigh"
       No tune given but intended to be sung

1109. Whither, oh! whither is my Lord departed
       11. 11. 11. 7   10 sts.   [Christopher Harvey]
       1640 The Synagogue, pp. 21-22

1110.   Who can number all the stars
             C. M. D.   4 sts.   [Thomas Shepherd]
             C. M.   1 st.
          1693 Penetential Cries, No. VII, p. 13
          No tune given but intended to be sung

1111.   Who grasp'd the Zodiac in his hand
             See: A comet dangling in   Jeremy Taylor
                the air

1112.   Who is the honest man
             6.10.10.8.10   7 sts.   George Herbert
          1633 The Temple, pp. 63-64
          1754 C.H.C.G., p. 218
          Begins: "The constant Christian still doth good
             pursue"
          Tune to be selected by meter from appended
          Table of Metres and Tunes

1113.   Who is this that comes from Edom
             See: Who's this we see from   Henry More
                Edom come

1114.   Who knows but such a one as I
             C. M. D.   6 sts.   [John Mason]
          1693 Penetential Cries, No. VI, p. 11
          No tune given but intended to be sung

1115.   Who knows, when he to go from home
             C. M. D.   4 sts.   George Wither
          1641 Hal. Pt. 1, No. XI, pp. 16-18
          Suggested tunes: Psalm 16 or 18

1116. **Who lives in love, loves least to live
             **C. M.   8 sts.   Robert Southwell
          **1634 St. Peter's Complaint, pp. 71-72
          1856 Reprint

1117.   Who would have thought, there could have been
             L. M. D.   6 sts.   Sir Henry Wotton
          1651 Reliquiae Wottonianae, pp. 534-536

1118.   Who would know sin, let him repair
             See: Philosophers have   George Herbert
                measured mountains

1119.   Who would true valour see

6. 5. 6. 5. 6. 6. 6. 5   3 sts.   John Bunyan
1744 (1st ed. 1684) Pilgrims Progress, Pt. II,
   pp. 155-156
*1873 Our Hymn Book: E. P. Hood, with tune,
   No. 398
*Begins: "He who would valiant be"

1120.   Who's this we see from Edom come
        L. M.   10 sts.   Henry More
        1668 Divine Hymns, appended to Divine Dialogues,
           pp. 500-501
        1828 Hys. of the P. E. Church, No. 61
        Suggested tune: Choice by meter

1121. **Whose soul is once betroth'd can ever be
        **10. 10   15 sts.   Seventeenth Century
        1754 C. H. C. G., Pt. I, No. 512, p. 296
        Tune to be selected by meter from appended
        Table of Metres and Tunes

1122. **Whoso hath rightly spy'd
        6. 6. 6. 6. 6. 5. 5
        1754 C. H. C. G., Pt. I, No. 349, p. 211
        Tune to be selected by meter from appended
        Table of Metres and Tunes

1123.   Why art thou, fainting soul, cast down
        L. M. D.   6 sts.   Richard Baxter
        1681 Poetical Fragments, pp. 79-80
        Suggested tune: Psalm 51

1124. **Why do I use my paper, ink, and pen
        **10. 10. 10. 10. 10. 10   3 sts.   Henry Walpole
        1588 Psalms, Sonets and Songs, No. 33
        Tune in same volume   William Byrd

1125.   Why do we seek felicity
        C. M.   9 sts.; Amen   John Austin
        1668 Devotions, No. III, pp. 33-34
        1671 Psalms and Hymns, with tune, p. 19
                                              John Playford

1126.   Why dost thou shade thy lovely face? O why
        10. 10. 10   16 sts.   Francis Quarles
        1635 Emblems, Book III, No. vii, p. 149
        st. 3, ℓ. 1: "Thou are my life: if thou but
           turn away"

1931 Songs of Praise, with tune, No. 670
                                      M. von Lowenstern
        Begins: "Thou are my life; if thou but turn away"

1127.   Why live I mudling here
              6. 8. 6. 8. 4. 4. 6. 4. 4. 6   8 sts.   George Wither
         1641 Hal. Pt. 1, No. LVII, pp. 100-103
         Suggested tune: In sad and ashy weeds

1128. **Why, O my brother, art thou sad
              **C. M.   19 sts.   [Sixteenth Century]
         1754 C. H. C. G., Pt. I, No. 426, pp. 248-249
         Tune to be selected by meter from appended
         Table of Metres and Tunes

1129.   Why shall I fondly treat this lump of clay
              10. 10. 10. 10. 10. 10   8 sts.   Lancelot Addison
         1699 Devotional Poems, pp. 71-74
              st. 2, ℓ. 1: "With too deep relish never let
              me like"
         1754 C. H. C. G., Pt. I, No. 519, pp. 298-299
              10. 10. 10. 10. 10. 10   3 sts.
         Begins: "With too deep relish never let me
              like"
         Tune to be selected by meter from appended
         Table of Metres and Tunes

1130.   Why should I grieve that I was made
              C. M. D.   7 sts.   George Wither
         1641 Hal. Pt. 1, No. IX, pp. 13-15
         Suggested tunes: Psalm 14 or 15

1131.   Why should my heart repine at those
              C. M. D.   4 sts.   George Wither
         1641 Hal. Pt. 1, No. CIII, pp. 203-204
         Suggested tune: Psalm 4

1132.   Why should unchristian censures pass
              L. M. D.   4 sts.   George Wither
         1623 Hymns and Songs, No. LXXV, p. 52
         Tune in same volume: Song 44
                                          Orlando Gibbons

1133.   Wilt thou forgive that sin where I begun
              10. 10. 10. 10. 8. 4   3 sts.   John Donne
         *1621 Sung at St. Paul's Cathedral
         1633 Poems, p. 350

1688 <u>Harmonia Sacra,</u> with tune, pp. 51-52
                                    Pelham Humphreys

1134.   With all the power my poor heart hath
            54 decasyllables   Richard Crashaw
         1648 <u>Steps to the Temple,</u> pp. 74-75

1135.   With all the pow'rs my poor soul hath
            L. M.   6 sts.   John Austin
         1668 <u>Devotions,</u> No. XVIII, pp. 160-161
         1701 <u>Devot. ed. H.</u>, p. 209; tune p. 2, separate
            section
         1754 <u>C. H. C. G.</u>, Pt. I, No. 402, p. 231
            L. M.   6 sts.
            Tune to be selected by meter from appended
            <u>Table of Metres and Tunes</u>

1136.   With bended knee and aking eyes
            See: With sick and famished   George Herbert
               eyes

1137.   With glory and with honor now
            C. M. D.   2 sts.
         1579 <u>The Psalms of David in English,</u> p. 75
            Tune in same volume: <u>Psalm CXLIX</u>
                                    William Damon

1138.   With humble boldness, trembling joy
            C. M.   8 sts.   Joseph Stennett
         1697 <u>Hys. in Commem.</u>, No. IX, p. 10
            No <u>tune given but intended</u> to be sung

1139.   With me, in me, live and dwell
            See: Welcome sweet and   George Herbert
               sacred cheer

1140. **With my poor off'ring be well pleas'd sweet Lord
            **14 decasyllables   Barnaby Barnes
         **1595 <u>A Divine Centurie of Spirituall Sonnets</u>
            1815 <u>Reprint,</u> p. 47

1141.   With Isr'el we may truly say
            8. 8. 8. 8. 8. 8   8 sts.   George Wither
         1623 <u>Hymns and Songs,</u> No. LXXXII, p. 56
            Tune in same volume: <u>Song 9</u>
                                    Orlando Gibbons

1142.   With sick and famished eyes

6. 8. 4. 4. 8. 2   14 sts.   George Herbert
1633 The Temple, pp. 142-145
1688 Harmonia Sacra, with tune, pp. 22-24
                                      Henry Purcell
1737 Collection of Psalms and Hymns, No. XVI,
     p. 52
8. 8. 8. 8   12 sts.
Begins: "With bended knees and aking eyes"
No tune given but intended to be sung

1143.   With too deep relish never let me like
        See: Why shall I fondly   Lancelot Addison
           treat this lump of clay

1144.   With what bounty and rare clemency
        See: Lord, with what   George Herbert
           bountie and rare clemencie

1145.   Ye holy angels bright
        6. 6. 6. 6. 4. 4. 4. 4   16 sts.   Richard Baxter
        1681 Poetical Fragments, pp. 84-88
        Suggested tune: Psalm 148

1146.   Ye that have spent the silent night
        See: You that have spent   George Gascoigne
           the silent night

1147.   Yet God's must I remain
        See: He that his mirth   Robert Southwell
           hath lost

1148.   You that enjoy both goods and land
        C. M. D.   7 sts.   George Wither
        1641 Hal. Pt. 3, No. XL, pp. 434-436
        No tune given but intended to be sung

1149.   You that have spent the silent night
        C. M. D.   10 sts.   George Gasciogne
        1575 Posies in section called Flowers p. xxi-
           xxiiii
        1897 The Westminster Abbey Hymn Book, with
           tune, No. 10   Samuel Reay

1150.   You, that, in children fruitful are
        L. M. D.   8 sts.   George Wither
        1641 Hal. Pt. 3, No. XV, pp. 378-380
        No tune given but intended to be sung

1151.   You, that like heedless strangers pass along
            10.10.10.10.10.10   16 sts.   George Wither
          1623 Hymns and Songs, No. LV, p. 42
          Tune in same volume: Song 24
                                                   Orlando Gibbons

1152.   You that regardless, pass along
            L. M. D.   15 sts.   George Wither
          1641 Hal. Pt. 2, No. XXXV, pp. 293-297
          Suggested tune: Psalm 51

1153.   You that the holy Jesus love
            C. M.   8 sts.   Joseph Stennett
          1697 Hys. in Commem., No. XXX, p. 39
          No tune given but intended to be sung

1154.   You that with just Zacheus do desire
            irreg.   5 sts.   Lancelot Addison
          1699 Devotional Poems, pp. 75-76
          st. 3, ℓ. 1: "Whatever others do intend to do"

1155.   You who our Lord's great banquet share
            C. M.   8 sts.   Joseph Stennett
          1697 Hys. in Commem., No. VII, p. 7
          No tune given but intended to be sung

1156.   Youth is a wild, a wanton thing
            8.6.8.6.4.4.6.4.4.6   6 sts.   George Wither
          1641 Hal. Pt. 3, No. XLV, pp. 444-446
          No tune given but intended to be sung

1157.   Zeal to God Almighty's praise
            7.7.7.7.7.7.7.7   9 sts.   George Wither
          1641 Hal. Pt. 3, No. XXVI, pp. 403-406
          No tune given but intended to be sung

BIBLIOGRAPHY

HYMNALS AND PSALTERS (Chronologically Arranged)

Sternehold, Thomas, Hopkins, Jhon, and others. The first parte of the Booke of Psalmes, collected into English Metre,.... conferred with the Hebreu, with apte notes to singe them withall. London: Jhon Daye, [1559]. (Boston Public Library **Benton 16. 01. 1)

Hopkins, John and others. The Residue of all David's Psalms in metre, with apt notes to syng them withal. London: John Daye, 1562. (Boston Public Library **Benton 16. 01. 1)

Damon, M. William. The Psalmes of David in English meter, with Notes of foure partes set unto them, by Guiliemo Daman, for Iohn Bull, to the use of the godly Christians.... Anno. 1579. London: Printed by John Daye. (British Museum K. 4. c. 5)

Byrd, William. Psalmes, Sonets, and songs of sadness and pietie, made into musicke of five parts. Superius Part Book. Printed by Thomas East, the assigne of W. Byrd, and are to be sold at the dwelling house of the said T. East, by Paules wharfe, 1588.

Damon, M. William. The second Booke of the Musicke of M. William Damon, late one of her maiesties Musitions: conteining all the tunes of Davids Psalmes, as they are ordinarily soung in the Church: most excellently by him composed into 4 parts. In which Sett the highest part singeth the Church tune. Published for the recreation of such as delight in Musicke By W. Swayne Gent. Printed by T. Este, the assigné of W. Byrd. 1591. (British Museum K. 7. a. 3)

Hunnis, William. Seven Sobs of a Sorrowfull Soule for Sinne. 1597.

_____. A Handfull of Honisuckles. Printed by Peter Short, 1597.

143

_____ . The Poore Widowes Mite.   Newlie printed by
Peter Short, 1597.

_____ . Comfortable Dialogs between Christ and a Sinner
. . . A Conflict betweene the spirit and the flesh . . .
Humble sutes of a sinner . . . A Lamentation . . .
A Psalme of reiosing . . . A Christian confession
. . . Praiers for the good estate of the Queenes
Highness.   1597.

Wither, George.   The Hymnes and Songs of the Church.
London: Assignes of George Wither, 1623.

_____ . Halelviah or Britans Second Remembrancer,
bringing to Remembrance . . . Meditations advancing
the glory of God, in the practice of Pietie and Vertue;
and applyed to easie Tunes, to be Sung in Families,
Composed in a three-fold volume.   London: Printed
by I. L. for Andrew Hebb at the Bell in Pauls Church-
yard, 1641.

Playford, John.   Psalms and Hymns in Solemn Musick of
Foure Parts On the Common Tunes to the Psalms in
Metre: Used in Parish-Churches.   London: Printed
by W. Godbin for J. Playford, 1671.

_____ . The Whole Book of Psalms: with The Usual
Hymns and Spiritual Songs; to-gether with the ancient
and proper Tunes sung in Churches... London:
W. Godbin for the Company of Stationers, 1677.
(Houghton Library,   Mus. 489.1677)

[Mason, John] Spiritual Songs, or Songs of Praise to Al-
mighty God Upon several Occasions.   Together with
The Song of Songs Which is Solomons.   London:
Printed for Richard Northcott Adjoyning to St. Peters
Alley in Cornhil, and at the Marriner and Anchor,
upon New-Fifth-street-Hill, near London Bridge, 1683.

Harmonia Sacra; or Divine Hymns and Dialogues: with a
Thorow-Bass . . . . Composed by the Best Masters
of the Last and Present Age.   The Words by Several
Learned and Pious Persons.   In the Savoy: Printed
by Edward Jones for Henry Playford, at his shop
near the Temple Church, 1688.

The Psalms and Hymns Usually sung in the Churches and
   Tabernacles of St. Martin's in the Fields, and St.
   James's Westminster. London: Printed by R. Ever-
   ingham for Ric. Chiswell, at the Rose and Crown in
   St. Pauls Church-yard, 1688. (British Museum
   A. 1230. ii)

Harmonia Sacra; or Divine Hymns and Dialogues: with a
   Thorow-Bass . . . . Composed by the Best Masters.
   The Words by Several Learned and Pious Persons.
   The Second Book. In the Savoy: Printed by Edward
   Jones for Henry Playford, 1693.

[Mason, John and Shepherd, Thomas.] Penetential Cries in
   Thirty two Hymns Begun by the Author of the Songs
   of Praise and Midnight Cry and carried on by another
   hand. Second edition. London: Tho. Parkhurst,
   1693. (British Museum 11641. aa. 13)

Hymns in Commemoration of the Sufferings of Our Blessed
   Saviour Jesus Christ Compos'd for the Celebration of
   his Holy Supper. By Joseph Stennett. London: J.
   Darby, 1697. (Royal School of Church Music, East
   Croyden, England)

Hickes, George. Devotions in the Ancient Way of Offices
   with Psalms, Hymns and Prayers... Reformed by a
   Person of Quality and Published by George Hickes,
   D. D. Second edition. London: 1701. (British Museum 3456. d. 38)

The Divine Companion being a Collection of New and Easie
   Hymns and Anthems for one, two and three Voices
   compos'd by the best masters, fitted and for the use
   of those who already understand Mr. John Playford's
   Psalms in Three Parts. London: William Pearson
   ...1701. (British Museum B. 655) Third edition 1715.

Lyra Davidica, or A Collection of Divine Songs and Hymns...
   And set to easy and pleasant Tunes for more General
   Use. London: 1708.

The Christian Sacrifice of Praise for the Use of the Religious
   Society of Romney, Collected by the Author of the
   Christian's Daily Manual. London: William Pearson,
   1724. (British Museum)

[Wesley, John] Collection of Psalms and Hymns. Charles-
      Town. Printed by Lewis Timothy, 1737. Facsimile
      Reprint with preface by the Rev. G. Osborn. London:
      T. Woolmer [1882]. (Royal School of Church Music,
      East Croyden, England)

A Collection of Tunes Set to Music, As they are commonly
      sung at the Foundery. London: A. Pearson, 1742.
      [Bound with Collection of Psalms and Hymns, 1737]
      (British Museum K.7.c.1.(2))

[Mason, John and Shepherd, Thomas.] Spiritual Songs: or
      Songs of Praise with Penetential Cries to Almighty
      God upon Several Occasions together with the Song of
      Songs which is Solomon's. 16th ed. corrected. Bos-
      ton: Green, Bushnell and Allen, for D. Henchman,
      1743.

A Collection of Hymns of the Children of God in all Ages
      . . . . Designed Chiefly for the Use of the Congrega-
      tions in Union with the Brethren's Church. London:
      Printed and to be had at all the Brethren's Chapels,
      1754. (Harvard University, 11427.754.)

Tate, Nahum and Brady, Nicholas. A New Version of the
      Psalms of David ToGether with some Hymns ... J.
      Stennett, Is. Watts, S. Browne and J. Mason as used
      in the English established church in Amsterdam And
      set to music by J. Z. Triemer. Amsterdam, Henry
      Gartman, 1772.

Belknap, Jeremy (ed.). Sacred Poetry Consisting of Psalms
      and Hymns Adapted to Christian Devotion in Public
      and Private. Boston: Apollo Press, 1795.

Psalms and Hymns for The Use of the Chapel of the Asylum
      for Female Orphans. London: J. Richardson, 1801.

Rippon, John (ed.). A Selection of Hymns from the Best
      Authors; Intended To Be an Appendix to Dr. Watts'
      Psalms and Hymns. 2nd Baltimore ed. Baltimore:
      Printed for Samuel Butler by John W. Butler, 1804.

Dobell, John (ed.). A New Selection of Seven Hundred
      Evangelical Hymns for Private, Family and Public
      Worship. Morristown: Peter A. Johnson, 1810.

Hymns Selected from the Most Approved Authors for the Use
of Trinity Church, Boston. Boston: Munroe, Francis,
and Parker, at the Shakespeare Bookstore, Cornhill,
1808.

A Collection of Psalms and Hymns, 2nd ed. New York:
David Felt, 1827.

Hymns of the Protestant Episcopal Church in the United
States of America. Boston: Massachusetts Episcopal
Missionary Society, 1828.

A Collection of Psalms and Hymns for Christian Worship.
Twenty-seventh edition. Boston: Charles J. Hendee
and G. W. Palmer and Company, 1839 [First edition
edited by Francis W. P. Greenwood, 1830]

Bickersteth, Edward (ed.). Christian Psalmody. Enlarged
ed. London: Staughton, [1841].

Martineau, James (ed.) Hymns for the Christian Church and
Home. 9th ed. London: John Chapman, 1852.

Adams, Nehemiah (ed.). Church Pastorals. Boston: Tick-
nor and Fields, 1864.

Selborne, Palmer Roundell, Earl of (ed.). The Book of
Praise from the Best English Hymn-Writers. Cam-
bridge, England: Sever and Francis, 1864.

Bickersteth, Edward H. (ed.). The Hymnal Companion to
the Book of Common Prayer. Annotated ed. London:
Sampson Low, Son, and Marston, 1870.

Hymns for the Use of the University of Oxford in St. Mary's
Church. Oxford: Clarendon Press, 1872.

Troutbeck, John (ed.). The Westminster Abbey Hymn-Book.
London: Novello, Ewer and Co., 1897.

Mackerell, Mrs. Perceval. Hymns of the Christian Centu-
ries. London: George Allen, 1903.

The English Hymnal with Tunes. London: Oxford University
Press, 1906.

The Book of Common Praise being the Hymn Book of the
Church of England in Canada. Toronto: Oxford University Press, 1908.

Ives, Charles T. and Woodman, Raymond H. (eds.).   The
     Institute Hymnal.   London: Novello and Co., 1913.

The Oxford Hymn Book.   Oxford: Clarendon Press, 1920.

Dearmer, Percy, and Others (eds.).   Songs of Praise. Lon-
     don: Oxford University Press, 1925.   Enlarged ed.,
     1931.

Gregory, A. E.   The Hymn Book of the Modern Church.
     London: Charles H. Kelly, [1931].

Shirley, F. J. (ed.).   The Hymn Book of the King's School.
     [Canterbury].   Oxford: University Press, 1947.

BOOKS

[Addison, Lancelot.] A Clergy-Man of the Country. Devotional Poems, Festival and Practical. London: Printed for Henry Bonwicke, at the Red-Lion in St. Paul's Church-yard, 1699.

Austin, John. Devotions, First Part In the Antient Way of Offices. With Psalms, Hymns, and Pray'rs; for every day in the Week, and every Holiday in the Year. Second edition. ROAN: 1672.

[Barnes, Barnaby] A Divine Centurie of Spirituall Sonnets. Reprinted from the edition of 1595. London: Longman, Hurst, Rees, Orme and Brown, 1815.

Baxter, Richard. Poetical Fragments: Heart-Imployment with God and Itself. The Concordant Discord of a Broken-healed Heart. . . . Written partly for himself, and partly for near Friends in Sickness, and other deep Affliction. London: Printed by T. Snowden for B. Simmons at the 3 Golden Cocks at the West end of St. Paul's, 1681.

_____. Additions to the Poetical Fragments. Written for himself. London: Printed for B. Simmons at the Three Golden Cocks at the West-end of St. Paul's, 1683. (Harvard University *EC 65. B3365. 681 p.)

Beaumont, Joseph. The Minor Poems. Edited by Eloise Robinson. Boston: Houghton Mifflin Company, 1914.

Breton, Nicholas. A Divine Poem, divided into two parts: The Ravished Soul; and The Blessed Weeper. London: for John Browne and John Deane, 1601.

[Browne, Sir Thomas.] Religio Medici. Printed for Andrew Crooke, 1642.

Brydges, Egerton (ed.). Excerpta Tudoriana: Or Extracts from Elizabethan Literature. 2 vols. Kent: Private Press of Lee Priory; by Johnson and Warwick, 1814.

Bunyan, John. A Book for Boys and Girls: or, Country
    Rhimes for Children. London: Printed for N. P.,
    1686. (Harvard University *EC65. B8865. 686b)

    _____ . The Pilgrim's Progress from This World to That
    Which Is to Come. The Second Part. 17th ed. with
    Cuts. Boston, N. E.: Printed by John Draper, for
    Charles Harrison, 1744.

Cecil, Lord David (ed.). The Oxford Book of Christian
    Verse. Oxford: Clarendon Press, 1940.

Coverdale, Myles. "Goostly Psalms and Spirituall Songs"
    in Remains of Myles Coverdale. Edited by George
    Pearson. Cambridge, England: University Press,
    1846.

Crashaw, Richard. Steps To The Temple, Sacred Poems,
    with other Delights of the Muses. London: Printed
    by T. W. for Humphrey Moseley, 1646. 2nd ed. 1648.
    (Harvard University *EC65. C8541. 646S)

[Crossman, Samuel] The Young-Man's Divine Meditations in
    Some Sacred Poems. London: Printed for Nath.
    Crouch. 1678. (Harvard University *EC65. C8848. 678 y)

Dighton, William (ed.). The Poems of Sidney Godolphin. At
    the Clarendon Press, 1931.

[Donne, John.] Poems by J. D. With Elegies on the Authors
    Death. London: Printed by M. F. for John Marriot,
    1633. (Harvard University STC 7045(A))

Farr, E. (ed.). Select Poetry, chiefly devotional of the reign
    of Queen Elizabeth. London: Parker Society, 1845.

Fellowes, Edmund H. (ed.). The Collected Vocal Works of
    William Byrd. Vol. XII, Psalmes, Sonets and Songs
    (1588). London: Stainer and Bell Limited, 1948.

Flatman, Thomas. Poems and Songs. London: Printed by
    S. and B. G. for Benjamin Took at the Ship in St.
    Pauls Church-yard, and Jonathan Edwin at the Three
    Roses in Ludgate Street, 1674.

Fleming, Abraham. The Diamond of Devotion, Cut and
    Squared into Six Severall Points. London: Printed
    for the Company of Stationers, 1608.

[Fletcher, Phineas] P. F. The Purple Island or The Isle
    of Man: Together with Pisactorie Eclogs, and Other
    Poeticall Miscellanies. Cambridge, England: Print-
    ers to the Universitie, 1633.

Gascoigne, George. The Posies . . . Corrected, Perfected,
    and Augmented by the Author. London: Printed for
    Richard Smith, 1575.

Gillman, Frederick John. The Evolution of the English
    Hymn. New York: MacMillan Co., 1927.

[Hale, Sir Matthew] Contemplations Moral and Divine. Lon-
    don: Printed by William Godbid, for William Shrows-
    bury at the Bible in Duke-Lane, and John Leigh at
    the Blew Bell in Fleetstreet neer Chancery-Lane,
    1676.

[Harvey, Christopher.] The Synagogue, or The Shadow of the
    Temple. Sacred Poems and Private Ejaculations in
    Imitation of Mr. George Herbert. London: Printed
    for Phil. Stephens, and Christopher Meredith, at the
    golden Lion in St. Paul's Church-yard, 1640.

Herbert, George. The Temple. Sacred Poems and Private
    Ejaculations. Cambridge: Printed by Thom. Buck,
    and Roger Daniel, printers to the Universitie, 1633.

Herrick, Robert. His Noble Numbers: or, His Pious
    Pieces, Wherein (Amongst Other Things) He Sings
    the Birth of His Christ: and Sighs for His Saviours
    Suffering on the Crosse. London: Printed for John
    Williams and Francis Englesfield, 1647. (Bound with
    Hesperides, London, 1648.)

Heywood, Thomas. The Hierarchie of the Blessed Angells.
    Their Names, Orders and Offices. The Fall of
    Lucifer with His Angells. London: Adam Inip, 1635.

Ingelo, Nathaniel. Bentivolio and Urania in Six Books. 2nd
    ed. London: Printed for T. Dring, J. Starkey, and
    T. Basset, and are to be sold at their Shops in Fleet-
    street, 1660.

Johnson [sic], Ben. Underwoods Consisting of Divers Poems.
    London: 1640.

Julian, John (ed.). A Dictionary of Hymnology. Revised
    edition with new supplement. London: John Murray,
    1907.

_____. Republication of Second Edition of 1907. New
    York: Dover Publications, 1957.

Keach, Benjamin. Sion in Distress: or, The Groans of the
    Protestant Church. [2nd ed.] London: Printed by
    George Larkin, for Enoch Proffer, at the Sign of the
    Rose and Crown in Sweethings-Alley, at the East End
    of the Royal Exchange, 1681.

Ken, Thomas. A Manual of Prayers For the Use of the
    Scholars of Winchester College And all other Devout
    Christians. To which are added, Three Hymns, for
    Morning, Evening, and Midnight. London: Printed
    for Charles Brome, [1715]

Kendall, Timothe. Flowers of Epigrammes. Included Tri-
    fles by Timothe Kendal Devised and Written (for the
    Most Part) at Sundrie Tymes in His Young and Ten-
    der Age. London: Imprinted in Poules Churche-
    yarde at the Signe of the Brasen Serpent, by Jhon
    Shepperd, 1577.

Milton, John. Poems, Upon Several Occasions. London:
    Printed for Tho. Dring at the Blew Anchor next Mitre
    Court over against Fetter Lane in Fleet-street, 1673.

More, Henry. Divine Dialogues. [with Divine Hymnes ap-
    pended] London: James Flesher, 1668.

Noyes, Alfred (ed.). The Golden Book of Catholic Poetry.
    New York: Lippincott Co., 1946.

Palgrave, Francis T. (ed.). The Treasury of Sacred Song.
    Oxford, Clarendon Press, 1890

Quarles, Francis. Divine Fancies, Digested Into Epi-
    grammes, Meditations, and Observations. London:
    Printed by M. F. for John Marriot, and are to be
    sold at his Shop in St. Dunstanes Church-yard in
    Fleet-street. 1632.

_____ . Emblems. Printed by G. M. and sold at John Marriots shope in St. Dunstons Churchyard Fleet-street, 1635.

Quarles, John. Divine Meditations upon Severall Subjects Whereunto Is Annexed Gods Love and Mans Unworth-inesse. with Severall Divine Ejaculations. London: Printed for the use and benefit of William Byron, 1663.

Shakespeare, William. Shake-speares Sonnets never before Imprinted. London: By G. Eld for T. T. and are to be solde by William Aspley, 1609.

Smyth, Richard. Munition Against Mans Misery and Mor-talitie. 3rd ed. 1634.

Southwell, Robert. The Poetical Works. Edited by William B. Turnbull. (Included "Maeoniae: or Certain Ex-cellent Poems and Spiritual Hymns." London, Printed by J. Haviland, 1634, and "Saint Peter's Complaint, Mary Magdalen's Tears, with Other Works of the Au-thor." London: Printed by J. Haviland, 1634.) Lon-don: John Russell Smith, 1856.

Spenser, Edmund. Amoretti and Epithalamion. London: Printed by H. L. for Mathew Lownes, 1611. (Harvard University fSTC 23084. 4)

_____ . Foure Hymnes. London: Printed by H. L. for Mathew Lownes, 1611. (Harvard University fSTC 23084. 4)

Tate, Nahum (comp.). Miscellanae Sacra: Or Poems on Divine and Moral Subjects. Vol. I. London: Printed for Hen. Playford in the Temple-Change, in Fleet-street, 1696.

Taylor, Jeremy. The Golden Grove, or a Manuall of Daily Prayers and Letanies. . . . Also Festivals Hymns, According to the Manner of the Ancient Church. Lon-don: Printed by J. R. for R. Royston, at the Angel in Ivie-lane, 1655.

Traherne, Thomas. The Poetical Works of Thomas Traherne, B. D. Now first published from the original manu-scripts. Bertram Dobell editor. London: 1903.

Vaughan, Henry. Silex Scintillans or Sacred Poems and Pri-
     vate Ejaculations. London: Printed by J. W. for H.
     Blunden at Ye Castle in Cornehill, 1650.

Vivian, Percival (ed.). Campion's Works. Oxford: Clar-
     endon Press, 1909.

Washbourne, Thomas. Divine Poems. London: Printed
     for Humphrey Moseley, at the Princes Arms in S.
     Paul's Church-yard, 1654.

Wotton, Sir Henry. Reliquiae Wottonianae. London: Printed
     by Thomas Maxey, for R. Marriot, G. Bedel, and T.
     Garthwait, 1651.

AUTHOR INDEX

(Numbers beside the name indicate entry numbers. Anonymous, Unknown, Seventeenth Century, etc., where used here, were found in the publication in which the hymns were printed.)

Addison, Lancelot
1632-1703
1, 20-22, 59, 61, 64, 67, 116, 125-128, 148, 153, 183, 185, 186, 217-219, 289, 314-316, 331, 347, 363, 376, 477, 598, 628, 630, 691, 714, 715, 727, 767, 795, 872, 907, 929, 993, 1027, 1050, 1063, 1064, 1097, 1098, 1129, 1143, 1154.

Anonymous
706, 916.

Austin, John
1613-1669
62, 65, 85, 87, 108, 114, 117, 121, 158, 159, 161, 162, 167, 168, 182, 195, 212, 293, 408, 409, 432, 435, 519, 559, 563, 573, 602, 611, 643, 653, 670, 801, 828, 878, 879, 891, 979, 999, 1011, 1013, 1014, 1125, 1135.

Austin, William
1587-1634
1028, 1034.

Barnes, Barnaby
1569?-1609
70, 77, 100, 101, 115, 177, 227, 228, 233, 239, 262, 319, 350, 367, 378, 597, 640, 690, 748, 763, 775, 793, 814, 818, 824, 832-834, 882, 924, 928, 997, 1002, 1008, 1140.

Baxter, Richard
1615-1691
44, 149, 151, 166, 203, 304, 490, 491, 517, 638, 647, 668, 1123, 1145.

Heywood, Thomas 1575-1641	31, 109, 355, 360, 373, 762, 953, 988, 990, 998, 1096.
Hunnis, William d. 1597	25, 32, 80, 98, 104, 243, 372, 441, 590, 593, 641, 716- 726, 728-741, 749, 756, 951.
Ingelo, Nathaniel 1621?-1683	1019, 1020.
Jonson, Ben 1573?-1637	10, 308, 709.
Keach, Benjamin 1640-1704	46, 344, 450.
Ken, Bishop Thomas 1637-1711	38, 41-43, 84, 118, 124, 206, 249-251, 312, 353, 364, 368, 518, 587, 589, 610, 760, 771, 1004, 1012.
Kendall, Timothy fl. 1577	371.
King, Rt.	585.
Marckant, John fl. 1562	755, 758.
Mason, John 1646?-1694	11, 26, 33, 47, 63, 83, 90, 113, 119, 122, 155, 156, 164, 215, 248, 254, 269, 306, 318, 323, 325, 336, 358, 359, 362, 390, 397, 404, 459, 474, 487, 520, 547, 564, 583, 599, 608, 609, 613, 619, 626, 627, 631, 636, 664, 688, 694, 754, 770, 776, 789, 862, 927, 931, 955, 957, 958, 963, 970, 972, 1029, 1032, 1043, 1099, 1114.
Milton, John 1608-1674	825, 943.
More, Henry 1614-1687	223, 252, 783, 798, 903, 909, 912, 1059, 1066, 1113, 1120.

Norden, John   908, 1044.
   1548?-1625

Norris, John   394, 449.
   1657-1711

Pestel, Thomas   105, 170, 216, 774.
   1584?-1659?

Quarles, Francis   152, 443, 633, 634, 781, 947,
   1592-1644   1126.

Quarles, John   18, 93, 94, 103, 181, 192,
   1624-1665   193, 202, 204, 234, 245, 246,
                      255, 256, 259, 261, 263-265,
                      267, 268, 270-275, 277, 278,
                      280, 281, 283-286, 310, 311,
                      320, 374, 383, 414-416, 419,
                      426, 429, 431, 433, 440, 453,
                      454, 456-458, 461-463, 465,
                      467-469, 472, 478-480, 482-
                      485, 489, 494-501, 503-505,
                      507-510, 512, 513, 515, 522-
                      531, 534-542, 550-555, 558,
                      561, 562, 567, 601, 612, 614,
                      620, 692, 693, 696, 698-704,
                      742, 750, 761, 785, 786, 788,
                      844, 846, 858, 874, 952, 959,
                      968, 989, 1036, 1038, 1095.

Seventeenth Century   144, 340, 386, 447, 464, 581,
                      584, 652, 772, 777, 838, 845,
                      913, 1006, 1056, 1083, 1121.

Shakespeare, William 809.
   1564-1616

Shepherd, Thomas   13, 27, 34, 54, 188, 221, 253,
   1665-1739   266, 343, 346, 352, 354, 548,
                      582, 595, 603, 607, 625, 743,
                      779, 780, 792, 875, 893, 921,
                      939, 960, 964, 983, 987, 1039,
                      1075, 1093, 1100, 1106, 1110.

Sixteenth Century   342, 683, 791, 799, 820, 977,
                      980, 1026, 1128.

Smith or Smyth, Richard   88.
  fl. 1609

Smith, Robert   92, 175, 403.
  fl. 1689-1729

Southwell, Robert   76, 96, 99, 172, 302, 357,
  1561?-1595   385, 427, 752, 769, 982, 1116,
                               1147.

Spenser, Edmund   579, 591, 682.
  1552?-1599

Stennett, Joseph   23, 45, 68, 69, 106, 163, 190,
  1663-1713   201, 237, 247, 257, 292, 295,
                               333, 337, 382, 384, 405, 411,
                               425, 470, 546, 560, 596, 639,
                               681, 744, 757, 802, 805, 822,
                               840, 855, 857, 892, 946, 992,
                               1025, 1040, 1047, 1086, 1103,
                               1138, 1153, 1155.

Stroud, W.   842.

Taylor, Jeremy   5, 17, 189, 191, 196, 222,
  1613-1667   225, 240, 241, 260, 276, 297,
                               298, 321, 356, 401, 448, 455,
                               475, 476, 502, 594, 637, 648,
                               678, 787, 813, 871, 899, 910,
                               938, 996, 1031, 1074, 1111.

Teate, Faithfull   19, 24, 178, 396, 580, 624,
  b. 1622?   657, 873.

Traherne, Thomas   877.
  1636?-1674

Unknown   160, 428, 712, 747, 898, 911,
                               1101.

Vaughan, Henry   29, 78, 82, 129-131, 157, 176,
  1622-1695   187, 379, 410, 413, 420, 423,
                               493, 569, 576, 600, 604, 642,
                               686, 708, 766, 796, 849, 926,
                               932, 1003, 1024, 1041, 1080,
                               1090.

973, 974, 978, 981, 984-986,
991, 994, 995, 1007, 1009,
1016-1018, 1022, 1030, 1033,
1037, 1042, 1045, 1046, 1049,
1053, 1054, 1058, 1060-1062,
1067, 1070-1073, 1076, 1079,
1081, 1084, 1089, 1092, 1102,
1105, 1107, 1115, 1127, 1130-
1132, 1141, 1148, 1150-1152,
1156, 1157.

Wotton, Sir Henry   205, 328, 784, 827, 1117.
  1568-1639

COMPOSER INDEX

Akeroyd, Samuel   184.
  17th Century

B.R.   695.

Bax, Arnold   549.
  1883-1953

Blow, John   60, 778.
  ?1649-1708

Briggs, George Wallace   572.
  1875-1959

Byrd, William   147, 326, 377, 697, 812, 1124.
  1543-1623

Calkins, John B.   635.
  [1827-1905]

Campion, Thomas   438, 650, 843, 1010.
  1567-1620

Clarke, Jeremiah   42, 86, 317, 339, 369, 659,
  18th Century   860, 1048.

Croft, William   307, 753.
  1678-1727

Damon, William   707.
  c. 1540-1591

Foster, Myles Birket   388.
  1851-1922

Gibbons, Orlando   2, 4, 8, 12, 40, 71, 95, 207,
      208, 230, 301, 335, 341, 380,
      402, 654, 655, 658, 804, 859,
      861, 889, 895, 896, 902, 936,

941, 945, 949, 973, 978, 984,
986, 994, 1017, 1062, 1071,
1072, 1076, 1089, 1132, 1141,
1151.

Händel Georg Friedrick   252.
   1685-1759

Holst, Gustav   360, 391.
   1874-1934

Houseley, Henry   595.
   1852-1925

Humphryes, Pelham   476, 1133.
   ?1645-1674

Hunnis, William   25, 32, 80, 98, 104, 243, 372,
   d. 1597   441, 590, 593, 641, 716-741,
                    728-741, 749, 756, 951.

Joseph, Jane   877.
   [1894-1929]

King, Robert   585.
   17th Century

Lawes, Henry   312, 591.
   1596-1662

Martineau, James   932.
   1805-1900

Playford, John   3, 108, 117, 152, 158, 161,
   1623-1686   212, 432, 559, 573, 602, 611,
                    670, 751, 801, 842, 1019, 1125.

Purcell, Henry   260, 671, 1142.
   c. 1659-1695

Reay, Samuel   1149.
   1822- ?

Shaw, Geoffrey   313.
   1879-1943

Turner, William   679.
   [1651-1740]

TUNE INDEX

166

Psalm 133   329, 839, 981.

Psalm 148   806, 987, 1039, 1145.

Psalm 149   1137.

Saint John   646.

Song 3   4, 40, 207, 335, 341, 532,
                       658, 861, 902, 984, 994, 1072,
                       1076.

Song 9   8, 95, 208, 654, 655, 896,
                       945, 949, 1062, 1071, 1089,
                       1141.

Song 24   1151.

Song 44   2, 71, 230, 301, 380, 402,
                       804, 859, 889, 895, 936, 941,
                       978, 986, 1017, 1132.

Song 47   12.

Song 67   1079.

Te Deum   35, 123, 210, 236, 460, 466,
                       488, 516, 644, 656, 663, 666,
                       851, 887, 967, 969, 985, 1033,
                       1054, 1067, 1073.

Ten Commandments   6, 49, 57, 139, 231, 242, 417,
                       481, 492, 605, 759, 823, 854,
                       869, 894, 935, 966, 1105.